REYKJAVÍK

Into the New Millennium

© Arctic Books
Kársnesbraut 63
200 Kópavogur,
Iceland.

Copyright is held by the publisher.

Printing: Oddi hf., Reykjavík.
Photo and photo-scanning: Ragnar Th. Sigurðsson.
Text: Ari Trausti Guðmundsson.
Design: Elísabet A. Cochran.
Translation: Martin S. Regal, Ari Trausti Guðmundsson, Mike Handley and Shelagh J. Smith.
Sumarliði R. Ísleifsson, Árni Hjartarson, Helgi M. Sigurðsson, Reykjavík Harbour, Reykjavík
Energy and Reykjavík Water Works added valuable input.

Reykjavík 2000

ISBN 9979-9275-3-4

REYKJAVÍK
Into the New Millennium

Ari Trausti Guðmundsson
Ragnar Th. Sigurðsson

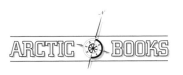

The Mayor's Address

Ingibjörg Sólrún Gísladóttir

Reykjavík is one of the Cultural Capitals of Europe for the year 2000. This is both an honour and acknowledgement for the city of Reykjavík and the Icelandic culture. Reykjavík, together with some of the greater, historical cities of Europe, was nominated as a Cultural City. This connection is a true privilege. As could be expected, this nomination has generated a great deal of activity on the cultural level by a wide array of organizers.

For the year 2000 many interesting cultural activities have been planned. I am not talking about cultural ceremonies for a small selected group, but rather culture in the wider sense of the word.

Moreover, venues for the cultural activities are being established or built, many of which will undoubtedly still be used in the future, namely the new premises for the Reykjavík Art Museum, the new headquarters of the City Library and other archives, the ambitious renovation of the National Museum, and the building preparations for the Art University of Iceland and last but not least, the recent decision by government and the City of Reykjavík to build a much sought after concert hall in the middle of Reykjavík.

The book "Reykjavík – Into the New Millennium" is one of the many projects for the Cultural City of the Year. The publishing of this book is in keeping with the theme "**Nature and Culture**" which has been chosen by Reykjavík for the Cultural City of the Year. It is expected that the book will contribute greatly to the introduction of Iceland, its nature and use of natural resources, especially the Greater Reykjavík area.

The founding of the Cultural Cities of Europe was established 25 years ago and one of the aims laid down by the committee was that cities, and countries, nations and ethnic groups introduce and display their distinct characteristics. This book can be seen as part of such an introduction to Iceland and especially Reykjavík, showing the unique harmonious existence of nature and culture.

In The Year of the Cultural City and at the turn of the century, great challenges await us which we can take to reinforce Icelandic culture both here and in the international arena. We must take full advantage of this opportunity.

Ingibjörg Sólrún Gísladóttir
Mayor

Into the future. *A solitary seagull takes to the air in front of City Hall.*

A banquet

A banquet. A play of forces that is an eternal offering in the world of nature known as Iceland. Venture there in good company, fearlessly and look deeply into how the primal elements gather momentum, producing a ceaselessly unfolding drama, alive before your eyes and set down in this book to prompt fuller, richer participation. Explore further the stage itself armed with this volume of knowledge, this guide to render thought more effective and understanding more receptive to spiritual pleasure. Let this help to satisfy your hunger as you make your way around the city of Reykjavík and all of Iceland.

Talking and writing about the approach of the millennium sometimes demonstrates either a hope or even concern that it will effect a clearly delineated break with all kinds of extra baggage, and that among the burdens it is destined to shuffle off is the book. What does this type of thinking involve? That people will wander like nomads about the earth, seeking to devour fast-food style messages found by instinct alone. The air is already trembling with such messages for all and sundry and mankind is on its way to becoming cyborgs. No more books. No more reflection. No more searching. No contemplation. An all-encompassing homogeneity.

The book offers other paths, paths that lead inwards, paths that take us into ourselves and the depths within us. At the same time, it shows us how to make the world our own by settling that inner country. It is an illuminated doorway that stands between the outer world of nature and the inner and provides a way to make exploratory voyages in both directions. It can speak to us of all time, fill history with moments of infinity, and absorb such moments into that short span which is a man's life. It can bring to life what happened millions of years ago, take us to stars that died in far off universes and make them flare up again in our minds as if still living. The book, for those in whom the embers of curiosity still glow, can help us to see into and through the present, offer us a symphony of the mind or a dividing of the waters to foster thought and wisdom. Unparalleled adventure. The book charts out its own routes, where each of us develops individual knowledge and wisdom, rendering us control over both. It quickens the imagination and the fruits of the imagination, continually nourishing the depths of our beings, continually offering us the whole world, enriching us, abating our hunger, quenching our thirst.

Thor Vilhjálmsson
writer

Thor Vilhjálmsson

Lavishly Illustrated Medieval Manuscript. *The ancient manuscripts and books of Iceland make a significant contribution to the literary treasures of the world. Iceland's famous writing tradition is carried into a new millennium.*

Fire

"The artist has to go beyond realism, broaden its scope, use it."

Erró

So said the artist **Erró** in an interview about himself and his work. He was slightly more reticent when he was asked: "Use it for what?"

Erró is the name adopted by the Icelandic artist **Guðmundur Guðmundsson** (b. 1932), who began his studies in Reykjavík in 1949. From there he continued to Oslo and then to Florence before travelling to various other schools of art all around the world. He settled finally in Paris 1958 and has been working there ever since. He is, by any standards, an extremely prolific artist.

Erró has engaged in many different kinds of work, including performance art, mosaics, film, collage, lithography, pen and ink and fresco painting, although most of his attention throughout the years has gone to oil paintings and water-colours. He is perhaps best known for his large, complex and eclectic oil paintings. Both the content and the style of his works are heavily influenced by the realist masters. Many of his paintings contain famous figures, caricatures, cartoons, consumer products, and sections from the works of other artists, carefully placed together in ambiguous, imaginative, provocative and yet accessible works. Erró frequently produces series and large mural works, several of which adorn public buildings in France. In 1989 the artist gave the city of Reykjavík thousands of paintings, documents and articles that span the entire length and breadth of his career. Known as the Erró Museum, it will officially open in a newly renovated branch of the Reykjavík Art Museum in the centre of town.

Erró has held a very large number of exhibitions throughout Europe, the US and in many other parts of the world, as well as in his native Iceland. He is now an internationally acclaimed artist.

*The painting **After burn** (oil on canvas, 162 x 97 cm, 1995) from the series **After burn pour Munoz** by Erró. All of the paintings depict a number of women, one of them central or prominent among the group. At the same time, each of the works also displays numerous ambiguous symbols, often surrounded with inscriptions. **After burn** allows the viewer to play with the meaning of the work, while the artist himself is usually reluctant to make any comment whatsoever on the question of interpretation.*

After burn.

Old roots

Since it is now generally accepted that Nordic people first came to settle in Reykjavík in the late ninth century, the year 2000 marks just over eleven hundred years of human habitation in this country. Yet nearly twenty million years have elapsed since increased volcanic activity along the North-Atlantic ridge formed the embryo of the land mass we call Iceland. Prior to that time, this area of the Atlantic Ocean, including eastern Greenland, the Faeroes and northern Britain, mainly consisted of other basalt formations created by the shifting of continental plates and vigorous volcanic eruptions.

The lowest stratum of rock in the Reykjavík area, however, is much younger than that, dating from about two to three million years ago. The bedrock mainly consists of bulky lava and palagonite tuff separated by thin layers of sediment. The uppermost stratum comprises a thick, rather old layer of plate lava (pahoehoe), covered by the most recent addition to the landscape, soil. This layer of soil is thickest in the various depressions and valleys in the Reykjavík area, but on the city's ridges and hills, the bare rock surface is made up of glacially scoured lava. Thus, the geological history of Reykjavík spans the beginning of the last Ice Age to the present day.

Lava Eruption (Krafla 1994). *Some 120,000 to 300,000 years ago, wide and long lava flows covered the Reykjavík city area. This lava constitutes much of the upper bedrock in that area.*

There is little visible difference between the dark basalt thrust up from volcanic eruptions in the last few years and that which forms the ancient basalt bedrock of Reykjavík. Both appear equally dense and sturdy, mainly because volcanic activity in Iceland has not undergone much change since the hot spot (mantle plume) associated with Iceland escaped the suppressing weight of Greenland due to the slow process of continental plate shifting. Then the hot spot began to pump more magma into the space between the plates and the ocean floor to form the island that much later attracted the adventurous Nordic settlers. For a long time the volcanically active rift area cut diagonally across the land mass from Snæfellsnes to Húnaflói. But several million years ago, activity began to subside there and a huge new rift system appeared in the east of the country, stretching from the south-west to the north-east where it still lies today. Where Þingvellir and Mosfellsheiði now lie huge volcanic centres, such as the famous Krafla in the north-east, appeared with their distinctive oblong fissure swarms.

The main volcanic centres erupted regularly and formed mountain massifs while eruptions in the fissure swarms poured layer after layer of lava onto the surrounding landscape. The ground was torn open by a succession of volcanic fissures, spewing up magma and incorporating dike injections that compensated for the average spreading rate of the plates which is about 2 cm each year. Over a period of a million years this volcanic activity created a 20 km thick land segment within the active rift zone in the south-west. Two to three million years ago, one of the products of these massive eruptions would have been a towering mountain in the area which is now Kollafjörður, north of Reykjavík. About one million years later, at the dawn of the Stone Age, when this central volcano had cooled, the activity of another volcanic centre formed the mountains and heaths that currently lie east of Mt. Esja, known as the Stardalur area.

Reykjavík and Vicinity. *In the forefront is Seltjarnarnes, an independent municipality. The landfills to the left include the former Örfirisey Island and protect the old harbour. The small bay southeast of the harbour is the original Reykjavík ("Bay of Steam") where the first settlements rose. The town of Kópavogur is to the right.*

Powerful Tephra Explosions *(Grímsvötn 1998). Many volcanic formations in the Reykjavík region include palagonite tuff layers, hills or mountains. They were formed in explosive, subglacial eruptions, chiefly during the last glacial period. Palagonite tuff is hardened tephra resulting from the rapid cooling and granulation of magma when it erupts into water.*

Subglacial Eruption (Grímsvötn 1998). *Numerous volcanic eruptions occurred beneath Ice Age glaciers on the Reykjanes peninsula. This is what the then subglacial Hengill central volcano could have looked like during an eruption.*

Meanwhile, the central volcanoes and fissure swarms drifted to the north-west and south-east, away from the magma sources within the active volcano rift zone of south-west Iceland. Later on, new volcanoes emerged within the presently active volcanic rift zone and new volcanic and tectonic activity continued the process of forming Iceland. Although the above-mentioned volcanic centres at Kollafjörður and Stardalur have long since cooled and become both inactive and heavily eroded, new centres have taken their place. One such centre is the relatively recently formed central volcano east of Reykjavík known as Mt. Hengill, which is only about two hundred thousand years old. However, aside from a few minor quakes, the Hengill volcanic system has lain dormant for nearly two thousand years. It erupts from time to time and volcanic fissures open up once in a while in the long fissure swarm which stretches to the north-east and south-west of the mountain. When the first settlers came to Iceland, they witnessed eruptions to the east of Reykjavík, close to Bláfjöll. Other active volcanic systems without prominent centres lie diagonally along the whole length of the Reykjanesskagi peninsula.

Still in the making

A pproximately 120,000 to 300,000 years ago, in periods when the Reykjavík area was not covered by glaciers from the last glacial Ice Age, large eruptions in the east poured numerous thin layers of lava plate over what is now Reykjavík. All the exposed basalt rocks in town date from this period, as well as those that lie just beneath the soil. While the land was periodically covered with Ice Age glaciers, successive eruptions created further strata characterised by palagonite tuff and breccias. All the volcanic craters that created those formations have now cooled down. During the last glacial period of the Ice Age (120,000 to 10,000 years ago), there were no active volcanoes within the Reykjavík area, though those in the Reykjanes peninsula were far from being dormant. Much of the central highlands and a number of mountains on the Reykjanes peninsula date from that period. Reykjavík itself has been free of glacial ice for about 10,000 years. During this time there have been no eruptions within what are now the city limits, though lava from eruptions outside the area has occasionally made its way inside.

"I think that the conditions facing a painter in Reykjavik are very good. The weather varies as do light and colours. You can observe the whole colour spectrum in the flora, fauna and the man-made environment. Nature also has an interesting effect on human activities, which are another source of artistic inspiration. Short days in winter are my main handicap – plus maybe the fact that the small community can sometimes prove repressive, especially in the professional arena".
Daði Guðbjörnsson, Painter

Lava Flows Beyond Reykjavík. *These lava flows from fissure eruptions in the Bláfjöll skiing area are between 1,000 and 4,700 years old. Even though danger of lava ever reaching Reykjavík is quite remote, there are active volcanic systems close to the capital. Across the Faxaflói bay, the Mt Snæfellsjökull volcano is clearly visible.*

Nevertheless, the Reykjavík environment is subject to constant change; rock strata to the east and the south of the city are still amassing from various eruptions and there is considerable rifting and subsidence due to plate shifting. Erosion and weathering, too, play a constant role. There is part of an active volcanic system only 15-20 km from the centre of Reykjavík, and only 7-8 km from the city limits to the nearest active crater at Búrfell. In addition to the Hengill Volcanic System, there are three other active systems along the Reykjanesskagi peninsula. Furthermore, the fissures and cracks in one of them, Trölladyngja Volcanic System, extend as far as eastern border of Reykjavík. None of these fissures has emitted lava since they are tectonic fissures resulting from earthquakes. This phenomenon is caused by the tension built up by plate shifting and means that those living in Reykjavík can occasionally feel the quakes that take place some distance away. There has been a number of volcanic fissure eruptions in the Trölladyngja Volcanic System over the past 10,000 years, the last of them occurring in the twelfth century, but the lava emitted from them never reached as far as the Reykjavík area.

Another volcanic system can be found at Brennisteinsfjöll, to the south and east of the city. There have also been a number of fissure eruptions there over the past 6,000 years, as well as one eruption from a shield volcano. Lava from those eruptions has extended as far as the present environs of Reykjavík, and on one occasion, long before the Settlement, all the way to the coast at Elliðavogur. The lava flows at Heiðmörk, a popular nature reserve close to town, are between 1,000 – 2,000 years old, while the last eruption in the Hengill Volcanic System dates back 2,000 years. In the thirteenth century, there was a submarine eruption off the Reykjanesskagi peninsula, in the most western part of the Reykjanes Volcanic System, which showered ash over Reykjavík. The remains of this eruption can still be seen in the soil and is known as the 'Medieval tephra layer'. The soil also shows evidence of tephra (i.e. ash and pumice) from much larger and more distant eruptions since the time of the Settlement, especially from Mt. Hekla and Katla as well as from the Vatnaöldur eruption in AD 870, which produced the 'Settlement layer' of tephra. Here, geological information indicated by different tephra layers in the soil strata is accurate enough to enable archaeologists to date various remains and artefacts found in that soil.

Movements of the earth's crust (tectonic rifting) are fairly common within the four volcanic systems on the Reykjanesskagi peninsula, producing frequent tremors that can be felt within the city itself. Earthquakes can reach as high as 5 – 6 on the Richter scale. Larger quakes (7 – 7.5), emitting from epicentres much farther to the east, can also be felt in Reykjavík, such as the one that occurred in 1896, though they are never likely to cause any serious damage from that far afield.

Man also brought fire

So, it is evident that fire, of subterranean origin, has formed the rock strata of Reykjavík and its environs over a long period of time, and is likely to do so, in one way or another, for the foreseeable future. Yet Man also brought fire with him, admittedly not as powerful as that inside the earth, but which has nevertheless had its effect on the

Birch and Rowan Trees*. The present city area was formerly covered to a large extent by shrubs and woods. Today reforestation not only brings back these old inhabitants but introduces foreign tree species as well.*

The Crust Splits Open. *Tension fissures in one of the four active volcanic systems on the Reykjanesskagi peninsula bisect the eastern suburbs of Reykjavík. They are an integral part of the fissure swarms associated with the above sea level section of the North-Atlantic Ridge. Tectonic movements along these fissures may cause earthquakes.*

Open Bonfire (brenna). Among other things, fire was widely used by Iceland's early settlers to forge iron. Nowadays, large open fires are seen on New Year's Eve and at summer solstice (Jónsmessunótt).

A Happy Dog and Happy Children. *Such a nice quartet brings to mind how good it is to be where kids smile.*

environment. The first settlers, who might have called this country Fireland or Greenland instead of Iceland, used fire for cooking and heating, but also for many other purposes such as forging, ship-building, ceremonial burials, sacrificing to the gods and consecrating land. Indeed, one of the methods for claiming land in the beginning was to light fires around the perimeter of the area being claimed in such a manner that each fire was directly visible from any other. And no sooner did the first settlers arrive in the bay now known as Reykjavík beside Laugarnes, with its clouds of steam rising from the hot springs in the Laugardalur Valley in the background, than they began to burn wood from the birch forests that covered the hills and heights of the town and take what land they needed.

The most ancient dwellings that have been excavated in Reykjavík show that they had wood-burning fire-places. Remains of charcoal and iron compounds reveal that fire was also used for extracting and forging iron. Moreover, it is highly probable that fire was used to some extent to clear forested areas and turn them into fields for crops and grazing as well as for building homesteads and farms.

All these fires were lit by people who could control its progress, but the same does not apply to subterranean fire. Today we can only imagine how the first settlers looked upon volcanic eruptions, but we do know that when lava flowed or ash fell in great volumes across inhabited areas, there was no way to stop it - any more than there is today.

Autumn. A proud, growing and man-made forest in Heiðmörk, inland to the east of the capital, is very popular for outdoor recreation activities.

From lava to geothermal heating

The first settlers in Iceland were predominantly Nordic people who were used to having plenty of timber at their disposal in their lands of origin. Yet Iceland's forestation could not have been as renewable and what trees and brushwood existed in the Reykjavík area was almost certainly depleted very soon after they arrived. Indeed, research on pollen found in Tjörnin (the city lake) and the marshlands beside it show that the number of birch trees in that vicinity suddenly declined in the tenth and eleventh centuries. Birch grows slowly in Iceland and has therefore never been an efficient source of wood for burning, which meant that the early inhabitants were soon forced to go farther inland to fetch wood. They also began to use both manure and peat for their fires. Peat is partially decomposed vegetation that has become densely packed, and could be found in the plentiful marshlands in and around Reykjavík, whence it was dug up with a spade or fork, split up into thin layers and dried. Neither peat nor manure is particularly good fuel but the inhabitants had little else to

"I was born and bred in Reykjavík. My shop is on Bankastræti – and my home is close by in a charming part of the old town. I really cherish living and working in the heart of the city and being able to simply stroll to concerts, theatre performances, movies and to those restaurants I like so much – all within just a short walking distance. I simply love my city, my Reykjavík!"
Erla Þórarinsdóttir, Clothing Shop Owner

choose from after the trees began to disappear. The situation was further exacerbated by a general drop in the annual temperature, as well as by the inevitable depletion of vegetation caused by over-grazing.

There are no coal mines in Iceland, and coal only began to be imported into the country in small quantities in the eighteenth century. However, slowly but surely, it became the principal fuel in Reykjavík as it turned from a village into a town. This use of coal continued into the first decades of the twentieth century, and on those days when the air was still, a familiar thick black smoke hung over the town. Shortly after the Second World War, coal began to be replaced by oil in some parts of the town, but the smoke was just as dense. Until the middle of the century, other fuels, such as paraffin and coke were all used, and the Reykjavík gasworks also played a vital role in the town's life.

Quite a number of small electricity plants appeared in the early years of the twentieth century, but the first of any size (by Icelandic standards) was the one constructed at the Elliðaár river in 1921, the same year as Rafmagnsveita Reykjavíkur (Reykjavík Electricity) was founded. To begin with, the electricity produced was used for lighting and industry within the town, but then a new form of energy was harnessed that came to revolutionise both domestic heating and the entire Reykjavík environment. This was the use of geothermal water, known as "hitaveita" in Icelandic, which was piped from beneath the surface of the earth directly into people's homes.

Hot Spring. *Hot springs and lukewarm pools existed in Reykjavík from the earliest of times, in Laugadalur. The steam was probably the reason for the name Reykjavík ("Steamy Bay" or "Smokey Bay").*

The first drilling was carried out in Laugardalur, which was just inside the town's environs at the time (1928), and was supervised by Reykjavík Electricity. The purpose was to utilise naturally heated water to produce electricity. However, it soon became clear that this would be both inefficient and expensive, and a decision was made to direct the geothermal water directly into houses and offices. A new company was established, Hitaveita Reykjavíkur (Reykjavík District Heating), and in November 1930 the geothermal water system was ready for use. A pipeline, 3 km in length, was used to transport water at a temperature of 70-80°C to a system of radiators (not unlike those used for oil central heating) in the town's largest primary school. As the water cooled, it was piped from the radiators directly into the street drainage system. Natural hot water was also used directly as tap water for washing and bathing. It has a characteristic light smell, produced by its gaseous content and is therefore not suitable for cooking or hot beverages.

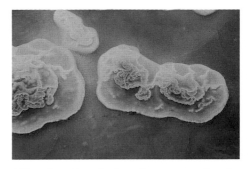

Silica deposits. *Geothermal water contains dissolved chemical compounds, gases – and solids like silica compounds. Hot, geothermal tap water may not be Iceland's tastiest – but it's harmless.*

Over the years following this experiment in geothermal heating, the National Hospital, Reykjavík's first indoor swimming pool, an additional school and about sixty private houses were connected up to the geothermal system, aptly enough from the very place where Reykjavík derives its name. Geothermal energy has proved to be an invaluable asset to the town. Aside from being relatively inexpensive, it produces no smoke or pollution, requires no domestic kindling and has significantly reduced the risk of damage by fire. At one and the same time, the development of this form of heating radically altered the Reykjavík environment for the better and places it in a very special position in today's world. What started in a few buildings now exists in every habitation in town and almost everywhere else in the country where geothermal water can be harnessed.

*A **Calm Cat**. This particular pussycat is either contemplating what to do about the birds on Tjörnin or is wondering how to land a solid job at City Hall.*

Sundhöllin Indoor Swimming Pool. *Reykjavík's geothermal water makes for delightfully warm swimming pools and hot jacuzzis! The oldest pool still in use is close to the old city centre. (Pool designed by Guðjón Samúelsson)*

Why geothermal energy?

Right from the beginning, settlers in Iceland knew about the geothermal energy below the surface of what is now Reykjavík as well as that found to the north of the town at Mosfellsdalur and Reykjadalur, and through the ages they used the hot springs and pools for washing and bathing. However, when the modern town of Reykjavík began to grow, this natural resource required sophisticated development.

Geological research and advanced technology made it clear that the Greater Reykjavík area contained several independent geothermal water reservoirs some 300 to 2,000 metres below the surface and in more places than was first realised, judging from the surface hot springs alone. The geothermal area at Reykir, 15 km north-east of Reykjavík, seemed the most viable place to start, and drilling began there in 1935. The town's new hot water company, Hitaveita Reykavíkur, (Reykjavík District Heating) took on the drilling, sale and distribution of the resource and still does to this day, although it has now merged with the Reykjavík Electricity to form Orkuveita Reykjavíkur (Reykjavík Energy).

In 1939, a double pipeline was laid between Reykjavík and Reykir, and the first storage tanks were constructed at Öskjuhlíð, close to the centre of town, in 1940. At the same time, work began on the construction of a giant underground hot-water distribution system beneath all the streets and into houses and buildings. The number of storage tanks increased to six, and placed as they were on one of the main hills, they became a prominent feature of the town's landscape. By the end of 1944, 2,850 buildings were connected up to the system, which fed water at a temperature of 86°C at a rate of 200 litres per sec.

What makes all this possible is that absorbed precipitation by the bedrock in the Greater Reykjavík area encounters a rock mass of between 100-300°C, constantly kept at high temperature by the ancient volcanic centres within the area and by magma beneath the active volcanic zone to the east of the town. Both old and more recent fissures determine where the reservoirs are located. There are many places where groups of cracks and fissures as well as good aquifers are easily exploited and hot water can be accessed by drilling to a

"To live in this city is a completely different experience, like an exciting adventure. I breathe the pure and clear air and forget the brawl and the noise of the world's metropolises. Here, people work with dedication and in unity, in harmony with God's great work: the magnificent nature. Working with other people, I learn something new every day and I feel that I am welcome. I feel the warmth in the hearts of Icelanders, who are tolerant and humanitarian. In return, I offer them the chance to share in the faith, hope and joy that reside within me."

Maria Guadalupe Gallegos
Nurse from the Order of Santa Margarita Maria, Mexico.

Geothermal Pipelines. *The total length of the main geothermal pipelines in Reykjavík is about the same as the distance around Iceland on the main road ("Ring Road") – about 1,400 kilometres. The pipelines are well insulated before they are buried. Very little heat is lost before the water enters buildings and homes.*

Grafarholt Geothermal Storage Tanks. *Plentiful, almost pollution-free hot water ensures that neither oil nor electricity is needed to heat houses and buildings in the Greater Reykjavík area. View to the southwest.*

depth of between 500-2,000 metres. The bore holes are lined with pipes, 15-23 cm in diameter, and pumps are used to carry the hot water both to each local pumping and distribution centre as well as to large storage tanks. Some of the precipitation flows down into the geothermal systems within the Reykjavík area and is heated there locally, but precipitation also finds its way into the reservoirs at deeper levels from much more distant areas. The geothermal systems at the roots of old volcanic centres, such as that at Laugarnes are hotter (130°C) than most of the other reservoirs and therefore contain more dissolved compound deposits (of which silica is the most common), and the characteristic pungent sulphurous smell is more obvious. The water is free of all bacteria and contains only small amounts of calcium. This makes the water 'soft' and therefore good for washing.

Swimming Lessons. All Icelandic pupils have mandatory swimming lessons and have to pass a minimum skill level.

What is "hitaveita"?

It requires substantial expertise and sophisticated equipment to find suitable geothermal fields, harness their energy, exploit the resource efficiently, understand what the environmental effects might be and then distribute the hot water to its destination. Iceland has developed geothermal research and technology for over half a century and is now a world leader in this area. The main centres for such research in Reykjavík are at Reykjavík Energy, the University of Iceland, the Energy Authority and the UN Geothermal Training Programme, which trains experts from all over the world.

All of Reykjavík (pop. 107,000 in 1998), and about 90% of the country as a whole, uses geothermal energy and Reykjavík Energy also manages the hot water resource for all the towns to the north and south of the capital (total pop. 50,000). For ordinary domestic geothermal heating the requirements are wells, pumps, a distribution system and a closed pipe- and radiator system leading into the buildings that are to be heated. Generally, the water used domestically is maintained at a temperature of about 80°C. By the time it leaves each house or building, it has cooled to about 30°C as it commonly runs, through the sewer system into the sea. Special radiator thermostats are used to regulate inflow of water in order to optimise usage. Geothermal water is also used for other purposes than domestic heating and waste water is often piped underneath pavements and parking lots to prevent them from icing over during the winter. Air and sea pollution from this resource is considerably lower than that coming from most other forms of energy.

"Despite our fast-moving society and even some stress that characterizes any urban community, Reykjavik has a lot to offer. We have a lot of different jobs and all kinds of services here, with health care of course being the most important. The city is a friendly place for children and young people. There are many leisure and creative activities at hand, which makes steering kids easier than one might expect. We also have more educational opportunities here than anywhere else in Iceland".

Marta Karlsdóttir, Teacher

The Pearl. *This stylish building houses restaurants, exhibition spaces and a panoramic balcony – all on top of the geothermal water reservoir tanks at Öskjuhlíð. A powerful, man-made geyser was recently introduced nearby. Shortly after the end of the last glacial period, Öskjuhlíð became an island – the result of a rising sea level that reached 43 m above the present one.*

The hot water is sold either by volume (in cubic metres or tons) or purchased in advance for a specific rate of flow (on average, 0.5-1.0 litres per sec.). The former method is used in Reykjavík and the average household's expenditure for heating and washing is about IKR 2,000-2,500 a month (1998). Per capita consumption is approximately 1,100 litres per day, and that includes both domestic and industrial heating. This means, for example, that heating costs in Iceland are nearly three times less than in Finland and five times less than in Denmark. This has meant an enormous saving on the cost of importing alternative fuels for heating (such as oil) and, at the same time, allowed electricity resources to be directed to other purposes than domestic heating.

From Laugardalur to Nesjavellir

I n 1984, when just less than fifty wells in the geothermal areas of Mosfellsbær and Reykjavík had been exploited to full capacity and all the neighbouring areas connected up to those sites, it was clear that new areas would have to be developed. The nearest large geothermal area to the east of Reykjavík is part of the volcanic centre at Mt. Hengill. There are two or three magma chambers heating large geothermal systems so that the reservoirs are made capable of being tapped for steam rather than hot water. A 1,800 metre deep well was sunk at Nesjavellir in 1982, right beside the volcanic fissure to the north-east of Mt. Hengill, active some 2,000 years ago. The temperature of the well exceeds 300°C and exerts enormous steam pressure. Of course, it is not possible to use burning hot steam directly for domestic heating, but Iceland has developed the technology necessary to solve this problem. The steam and condensed water are used instead to heat fresh cold water from shallow bore holes in specially designed heat exchangers. The heated water is then distributed to the consumer, but condensed water is partly led back into the bedrock. A proportion of the steam can be used to produce electricity with steam-powered turbines.

A large water- and electricity plant has been constructed at Nesjavellir. Eighteen deep holes were drilled there, over half of them in current use. In 1990, this site produced about 100 MW of extra power for Hitaveita Reykjavíkur. The water was at a temperature of 80°C and flowed at 560 litres per second along 27 km of pipeline to the capital. All the pipelines are above the surface of the ground and are so well insulated that the temperature of the water decreases by no more than 2-3°. The power capacity was increased again in 1992 to 150 MW, though its potential is as much as 400 MW and could remain at that level for thirty years, should such capacity be needed in the future. In 1998, the Nesvellir Power Plant began to produce electricity (2 x 30 MW), using steam and its capacity to heat water increased to 200 MW (1,100 litres per sec.).

At the turn of the millennium, Reykjavík wil be able to boast of an environmentally friendly domestic heating system. The annual consumption of hot water for the entire area managed by Reykjavík Energy is 58-60 million tons and is distributed to nearly 40,000 homes. The pipelines used for this have now reached a total length of more than 1,400 km, which is roughly approximate to Highway 1 that circumscribes the country. The entire production, distribution and invoicing systems are computerised. About one third

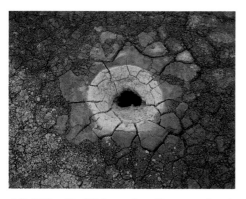

A Bubbling Mud Volcano (a solfatara mud pot). *A small steam and mud vent at the Nesjavellir geothermal area resembles a volcano from above. Underneath it, the temperature exceeds 300- 400°C at a depth of 2,000 m.*

Drilling Rig Control Panel. *The most efficient geothermal drilling rigs sink wells 2,000-3,000 m into the earth's crust, be it vertically or diagonally.*

Laugarnes. *One of the Reykjavík outposts, rising from the sea. This small peninsula was once the site of one of Reykjavík's main farms. It is currently a protected nature reserve and archaeological site.*

An Untiring Drilling Crew. *Without drilling techniques, Iceland's enormous geothermal resources would be of little use. The Icelanders have become experts in geothermal drilling as well as steam or water reservoir exploitation. They are busy at home and abroad. Most wells are 500 to 2,500 m deep but a 3,080 m dry well has been sunk in Reykjavík.*

Nesjavellir Geothermal Power Plant. *This is the newest addition to Reykjavík Energy. The plant produces hot water by using steam to heat cold groundwater in special heat exchangers. Electric power is produced as well, with steam turbines. This geothermal activity comes from heat stored within the Hengill central volcano.*

Violet Dreams...In the lyrics of a popular Icelandic song, Mt. Akrafjall (left) and Mt. Skarðsheiði (middle) are likened to violet dreams on a beautiful summer night. Mt. Esja is seen to the right.

of the hot water comes from systems within the city, one third from Mosfellsbær and the final third from the Nesjavellir area. There are now storage tanks in three places. The first group is at Öskjuhlíð, where five such tanks containing 24,000 tons of hot water support the glass dome known as the Pearl, an exhibition hall and restaurant. The second group, containing 54,000 tons is at Grafarholt, and the last and smallest group at Reynisvatnsheiði where some 18,000 tons are stored.

Bathing in geothermal water

Elliðaárdalur Power Plant. One of the oldest still operable electric power plants in Europe is in Reykjavík. It provided the town with electricity in the 1920s and for decades after that.

Hot water for swimming pools and health resorts is a luxury in most countries, where the water has to be heated either by electric or oil power. Yet in Iceland, the geothermal resources in most parts of the country mean not only that people have an abundant supply for space heating, but that it is also possible to have more than one hundred swimming pools in the vicinity of the geothermal areas.

The City of Reykjavík operates six such swimming pools, four outdoor and two indoor. All of these also contain various other facilities, such as outdoor jacuzzis, steam rooms and saunas and small recreation centres. They are visited by thousands of people each day, summer and winter, and swimming is a compulsory part of the curriculum in all schools. The entrance fee is inexpensive, and most people fully realise how important a role these pools serve both socially and as far as health is concerned. It is not unusual to see various clubs or teams of athletes invade one of these pools for a good soak in the hot pots after several hours of exertion or to see prominent politicians and other public figures there engaged in intense discussion. One might say that they are the Icelandic equivalent of the ancient Roman baths.

There are plans to create a large hot water lagoon at Nesjavellir along with bathing and swimming facilities, not unlike the more famous bathing spot, the Blue Lagoon, an acclaimed geothermal and recreational centre close to the Leifur Eiríksson International Airport.

Wintry Outdoor Swimming Pools. *Swimming and exercises in water, all year round, are popular sports in Iceland. The geothermal water in the pools stays 28-30° C. Older people take advantage of Reykjavík's many pools and there are special sessions for them at the larger facilities.*

Earth

". . . a small sign concerning the uniqueness of the country and its people."

Finna Birna Steinsson

These are the words of artist **Finna Birna Steinsson** about her own work recorded in a programme accompanying the exhibition she held in the Ásmundar Gallery in the spring of 1996. This short comment encapsulates the essence of many of Finna Birna's works, many of which are sculptures that fall into the category of environmentalist art.

The works of **Finna Birna Steinsson** (b. 1958) largely examine the meaning of man-made structures and natural phenomena, and their interface and interplay which lead the viewer to contemplate both the country and its people. Unusual natural forms in the man-made environment, or the reverse, unusual man-made objects in the natural environment, have characterised much of her work. They are also often accompanied by short essays which contain the artist's thoughts on such matters. Many of the works are very large, for example, "1.000 veifur í Vatnsdalshólum," and Finna Birna commonly reproduces scaled down versions of some of them to fit into exhibition halls and galleries.

Finna Birna studied art in Winnipeg, Reykjavík and Munich, but settled back in Reykjavík many years ago and has been working there ever since. She has been the recipient of many awards and prizes both at home and abroad, and taken part in 17 joint exhibitions as well as having held 6 solo exhibitions.

Finna Birna Steinsson's great inventiveness is a mark of her originality.

*The work **Út um stéttar** ('Mounds') was first shown at Kjarvalsstaðir in 1994 and is a subtle combination of natural forms and modern architecture in a concrete environment. Concerning the mounds themselves in this work, the artist has the following to say: "they represent the interplay of the weather and the Icelandic landscape across the ages. One might think of them as being plump and fertile offspring of the marriage (hierós gámos) of heaven and earth in these northern climes. There are all sorts of indications that special characteristics of certain countries and peoples, especially among the smaller nations, will be flattened out or obliterated by the increasing international economic homogeneity and the mass media. These times of uncertainty are exactly the right moment to bring these mounds into the open to remind us of their mystery, energy and simplicity, the right moment to express roundness and wholeness once more".*

Út um stéttar.

Shaped by water

The landscape of the Reykjavík area is quite different today than it was when the large volcanic centres were active some 1-3 million years ago. Most of the highland area has now disappeared and two small fjords Skerjafjörður and Kollafjörður, mark the borders of a long peninsula comprising shallow valleys and low hills. This area is further surrounded by low hills, dales, moors, lava fields and lakes.

Erosion and weathering have taken their toll on the bedrock and soil and dramatically altered the mountainous landscape that once existed here. Most change, however, has been effected by water in the shape of heavy moving glacial tongues, the constant beating of the ocean on the shoreline and by fast-flowing rivers. Erosion and weathering have removed thick layers of rock formations, turned them to dust which has since been driven over land and into the sea. Weathering also dissolves the rock and the chemical compounds are absorbed by the ocean.

Glacial ice has probably played a major role in erosion. The Ice Age began about three million years ago in Iceland, and since then about twenty glacial periods, each lasting about 100,000 years, have ravaged the country. Most of the surface of the country disappeared under a thick sheet of ice which stretched far into the sea. Mountain summits jutted up above the ice cap and outlet glaciers eroded the bedrock and calved into the surrounding ocean. Where fast moving glaciers formed, they carved out valleys and fjords, and between them large mountains, such as Mt. Esja, were created. Where there were subglacial volcanic eruptions, the eruptions heaped up palagonite mountains such as Bláfjöll. In the much shorter, interglacial periods, layers of sediments settled and common lava was able to flow from the volcanoes and spread over the surrounding areas. At the end of the last glacial period, about 10,000-20,000 years ago, the landscape of the Reykjavík area slowly began to resemble what it is today. When the glacial ice retreated farther inland it left in its wake a trail of glacier-scarred bedrock, mud, sand, and moraines in the lowlands. This means that the Reykjavík area would have looked quite bleak as the current (Holocene) interglacial period started.

Should a new glacial period commence, Reykjavík would inevitably disappear under the glacial ice and the town would slowly but surely be pushed into the ocean. The closure of an interglacial period usually only lasts a few decades, and it would take glaciers only a few centuries to move from the highlands into the sea.

The sea has also shaped the landscape of what is now Reykjavík, and especially so since the end of the last glacial period. Indeed, these days the sea is the most powerful erosive force in the area. The continuously pounding surf breaks the rock face and bears the fragments into the bays and inlets, where it builds up sandy gravel beaches and sand bars. In the bay where the old harbour once stood, a gravel and sand bar closed off a small lake or lagoon. This is Tjörnin, one of Reykjavík's most distinctive features. The fresh water there comes from the surrounding hills and marshlands but when the tide is full it also

Nothing Prevails Forever. *Frost, water, wind and other processes of erosion and weathering take their toll on the Reykjavík bedrock.*

A Moving Glacier Tongue (Sólheimajökull). *During the glacial periods of the Ice Age, glaciers sculpted the landscape in and around Reykjavík. They also deposited glacial sediments, which still cover large bedrock areas.*

Mt. Esja. *This is the northern side of the Mt. Esja (913 m), the "town mountain." It is long and bulky, made of different rock types and is believed to be an eroded remnant of thick eruptive or intrusive formations from the outer regions of a central volcano which was active 2-3 million years ago. Many walking and climbing routes are found on the mountain.*

has a small intake of salt water. To the south-west of the bay, small islands were connected with the mainland by long rocky bars. The island of Örfirisey and the Hólmar islets became attached to the small peninsula west of the town lake. Actually, this is where Reykjavík's first merchants' stores were built in the sixteenth and seventeenth centuries. For a time, Reykjavík was known as "Islets' Harbour" by the Danes. At Örfirisey extensive land reclamation has changed the appearance of the area, and there are now factories and businesses where there were once only waves.

Coastal land subsidence has long been a problem in the south-west in general and Reykjavík in particular. The increasing amount of glacial melting all over the world has meant a corresponding increase in the volume of the oceans. The rise of the seaboard resulting from combined slow land subsidence and increased global annual temperatures is, on average, 0.3 cm a year at the present time and preparations are already underway to protect the town coastal areas from being constantly worn away by the ocean.

Flowing water has played a much smaller role in erosion over the past thousands of years as far as Reykjavík is concerned, although significant examples can be seen at the Elliðaár river, where waterfalls, rapids and old river beds.

The City of Children. *The annual population growth rate in Iceland has been 2-2.5%. Children are a common and welcome sight in the safe city of Reykjavík.*

Soil is a mainstay

Two other results of erosion and weathering ought to be mentioned. Firstly, wind and water erosion have swept away a lot of the soil, especially since the forests and shrubs disappeared during the first few centuries of Reykjavík's history, and the general over-exploitation of vegetation and deteriorating weather conditions have exacerbated the problem. In many places in the Reykjavík area, one can see soil stacks and patchy soil and even bare glacial moraine. For decades, people have countered this unfortunate development through this soil reclamation and cultivation. Indeed, over the past five or six decades, it is man who has played the greatest role in shaping the landscape. Almost the whole coastline of the peninsula has been changed. Hills, dales and fields have given way to housing development, streets, gardens, and parking lots. Almost all the marshland has been drained, and trees have been planted or grass sown on most of the open spaces that remain.

Secondly, continual freezing and thawing also produce considerable weathering, splitting and breaking of rocks, raising and shifting the soil layer,

"Reykjavík is like a teenager, not small anymore – and turning big. It's developing fast, untamed and far from being fully created, still spreading and growing but changing inside as well. This makes the city fresh and vivid. I think it's stimulating to live and work in such an environment".

Edda Andrésdóttir, TV News Anchor and Host

Volcanic and Glacial Soil. *Soil thickness in Reykjavík ranges between 10 cm and 6 m. The thickest soil layer is found in wet mires. The soil is composed of local glacial sediments, river and lake sediments, tephra layers and windblown dust containing clay and glassy volcanic deposits – and, finally, of organic material and minerals.*

and in many places fences, posts and whatever else has been driven into the ground, have been pushed up again.

From the late medieval period until about 1900, the climate in Iceland appears to have been somewhat colder and subject to more precipitation than at present. However, in the early 1920s, annual temperatures rose significantly and over the next few decades the weather was warmer than at any time since the first centuries after the Settlement. This was followed by another cooler period from 1965-1987, but annual temperatures then began to rise again and have continued to do so very slowly.

Yet despite erosion, weathering and the fluctuations in temperature during the relatively warm period since the last glaciation, the soil cover in the Reykjavík area has been reasonably adequate. No part of it is more than 10,000 years old. In the former marshland areas, usually at the base of valleys, the soil is up to 5-6 m thick, and in many places quite coarse-grained. On those hills and heights where there is not bare gravel or a glacially scoured lava surface, the soil layer is generally thin and dry, interspersed with windborne tephra and dust, and the marshland soil also comprises two layers of birch remains. These are from the two periods of thicker forestation, which reached their prime respectively nearly 8,000 and 3,000 years ago. Both in the marshlands and in drier soil there are thin layers of tephra.

The Tower. *This small building has been situated in a number of different places in the city centre since the early 20th century – housing, for example, a kiosk and a tourist information centre.*

Careful Cultivation

In the second half of the nineteenth and the first decades of the twentieth century, there were small gardens all over Reykjavík, used both for growing vegetables and for planting the first large trees to be imported into the country. In many parts of the old town, one can therefore still see leafy Danish maples and beautiful elms alongside the smaller native rowan trees. A small but charming garden was planted behind the Parliament Building in 1908, and another at the old churchyard on Suðurgata containing a fine assortment of trees.

From the 1940's onwards, the town authorities put considerable effort into increasing the number of gardens and open green spaces, and this trend was echoed in a new interest in gardening on the part of the townspeople themselves. Reykjavík now boasts a number of public gardens and parks, such as that at the south end of Tjörnin, at Laugardalur, at Fossvogsdalur and at Kjarvalsstaðar on Miklatún. In addition to these, there are many playing fields and sports grounds all over the city.

"Reykjavík is a great city to live in. The mountains and the glaciers are never far away. Most of my friends have the same need as my own – to tackle as many high summits as possible. The weather's never dull – never the same for very long".

*Árni Árnason, **Computer Specialist***

Greylag Geese at the City Centre Lake. *Reykjavík seeks to be known as a green, environmentally safe city. By long-term policymaking and action planning, industry, services and resource management will be handled in a sustainable way.*

Walkers´ Bridge at City Hall. *A fine view across Tjörnin to Tjarnargata, a street, lined with stately timber houses from the turn of the 20th century.*

Reykjavík – The Garden City. A cosy tree and flower garden at a typical, simplistic concrete house from the forties is one of thousands of similar, private home gardens in the city.

Austurvöllur: A small garden square in the heart of Reykjavík situated in front of Parliament House. A popular place for Reykjavíkians to relax a while.

Popular Cycling. *Bikes tend to be used for recreation rather than as means of transportation in Reykjavík. A network of walking and cycling paths covers the whole city.*

The town authorities decided long ago that Reykjavík should have an environment that was both green and artistically striking. In most open public areas one can see many sculptures and other large works, both by the nation's most famous artists and by many foreign artists as well.

The extensive private cultivation of trees, flowers and lawns has utterly changed the face of Reykjavík. Looking down from the various hills on to both the town and the suburbs on a summer's day, one can see how Reykjavík is almost a garden city. Among the plentiful conifers the most obvious are the Alaska spruce, Siberian larch and various varieties of fir, and of the many foreign deciduous trees, the Alaskan poplar is the most common.

In addition, many open spaces have also been used to cultivate woods, and native shrubs and bushes have been given the opportunity to flourish. Öskjuhlíðin, where the geothermal tanks stand, is an excellent example. Another can be found in the Elliðaárdalur valley, where much of the lava has been covered with trees and shrubs. On the slopes of Breiðholt and to the east of the town, for example at Hólmsheiði, thousands of trees have been planted to form a solid green border around the suburbs. But the largest wooded area is on the lava that once threatened to engulf the town but stopped at Elliðavatn. That area is called Heiðmörk and has acre upon acre of birch, fir and pine, amounting to no less than five million trees in all. When the weather is fine, people from Reykjavík can go to this now fertile, wooded area, carefully plied with walking paths, and enjoy the outdoor life. Both walking and cycling paths have been laid along the north and south shores of Reykjavík, and during the

"I live in Reykjavík. There are theatres and art exhibits within reach. I'm not always in a theatre but I can be whenever I want. I work in Reykjavík and my roots are here. I am the branch that strengthens the tree and Reykjavík resides in me".

Einar Thoroddsen, Medical Doctor

Man's Trusty Servant. *That's what the Icelanders used to call their horses. Today, thousands of privately owned horses call special stables in the Greater Reykjavík area their home. This unique, surefooted Icelandic breed is ridden along a good network of city horseback riding paths.*

winter most of the areas surrounding the city make good terrain for cross-country skiing. Skating, which has always been a popular activity in Reykjavík can now be practised at the new skating rink in Laugardalur and the more traditional location of Tjörnin, as well as on many other small lakes and ponds around the outskirts of the city. There is also a good golf course at Grafarholt in the eastern part of Reykjavík.

Rock, turf and timber

To begin with there were probably just four large farms in the Reykjavík area: the Settlement farm at the north end of the lake, at Nes on Seltjarnarnes, the farm (and soon after a church) at Laugarnes, and finally the farm on Viðey, the largest island in Kollafjörður, just 3 km off the coast. All four were traditional livestock farms, supplemented by some fishing, and they must have looked like most other farms scattered around the country. The main farmhouse was known as the 'longhouse' (skáli) and was surrounded by a number of smaller buildings, such as the smithy and various wooden sheds for storage. The longhouses were long but rather narrow buildings, constructed from timber logs and walled and roofed with turf and branches. More rarely, the walls were made of stone. The size varied considerably, but many had extensions that housed a larder, a sitting area and a cooking room. The longhouse contained the main fire as well as beds and some benches.

The quality of the land in the Reykjavík area deteriorated somewhat as it became more densely populated and smaller outlying farms began to appear along the coast and inland towards the Elliðaár river. At the same time, the larger farms began to diminish in size.

However, one of the main farms, on the island of Viðey, remained in a class of its own. A monastery was built there in the thirteenth century and Viðey soon became Reykjavík's centre of learning and culture. Indeed, the farm owned by the monastery became one of the richest in the country. At the time of the Reformation in the mid-sixteenth century, the wealthy Viðey monastery came under the Danish monarchy and later it became the residence of the Governor of Iceland. Previous to that, the Governor's residence had been at Bessastaðir which, after independence in 1944, became the official presidential residence. In the mid-eighteenth century, Skúli Magnússon was Iceland's chief represen-

"Reykjavík is a wonderful place for meteorologists, especially if you work as a forecaster. Most low-pressure systems are noticed here first. There are certainly enough of them — and with endless variety. Even if Reykjavík is the country's only real city, I always think of it as a conglomerate of small villages and I am lucky enough to live in one with my grocery store on the corner. Anyway, I am probably like many other people – I always feel fine when I'm in a beautiful place amongst good people. I've had fine neighbours, not too fussy towards petty incidents – like my young son's having buried their Christmas dinner, some ptarmigans, in our garden".

Unnur Ólafsdóttir, Meteorologist

Peat. *Old, pressed soil, rich in organic material (plant remains) was dug out of Reykjavík's mires for centuries and used as domestic fuel for fires and stoves. The peat was dried in the open. The finger is pointing at a small, few thousand year old birch twig in the peat.*

Aðalstræti 10. The oldest house in Reykjavík dates back to the latter half of the 18th century. It is now a pub and restaurant. One of the old freshwater wells is seen in the foreground.

tative to the Danish crown and it was he who was responsible for building up trade and business in a country which had depended almost entirely on subsistence farming. One of the many projects initiated by Skúli Magnússon was the Reykjavík wool trade. Magnússon has often been called the 'father' of Reykjavík and with good cause, and some of the buildings from that period are still on Viðey.

The old-style longhouse was slowly superseded by buildings made of turf and stone. These had much smaller rooms, low ceilings and long passageways. In the wealthier establishments, the gables and most of the interiors were made of timber. The longhouse was replaced by a living and sleeping room known as the *baðstofa*. Churches were either made of turf with wooden gables or constructed entirely of wood imported from Norway or Denmark. Some other buildings were also made of timber throughout, while the so-called 'stone' houses, made from either roughly hewn blocks or stone bricks, did not appear in Iceland until the eighteenth century when they were used for stores or public buildings.

Fresh Air at Suðurgata. Brass bands are a part of the Reykjavík scene, especially during festivals and public holidays.

New times, new architecture

Reykjavík was granted the status of a municipality on 18 August 1786. At that time, the township stood on a gravel bar between the lake and the sea and had a population of about 300. In the same period, the diocese of the Bishop of Iceland was moved from Skálholt to Laugarnes in Reykjavík, and a new cathedral and school erected in the centre of the capital. The Danish crown's chief representative or governor took up residence in Reykjavík in 1798 and the Alþingi (Icelandic Parliament) was moved there from its ancient location at Þingvellir. The Alþingi was abolished in 1801 and not reinstated until 1845, when it acted in a purely advisory capacity to the Danish authorities.

A number of large public buildings, such as Alþingishús (Parliament House) Amtmannshúsið, the town jail (now Cabinet House), Reykjavík Cathedral, and the Reykjavík Grammar School were all constructed in the last decades of the eighteenth and the first half of the nineteenth century. Cabinet House (Stjórnarráðshúsið), has a timber frame and timber floors while the walls are partly made of stone bricks. The cathedral, too, is made from both Icelandic and Danish stone while the grammar school is an entirely wooden construction. Many timber houses were also built during this period in among

"I'd travelled to 43 countries before I came to Iceland. Where had it been all my life! The most civilized, modern, safe, fun and magical country I'd ever discovered was to draw me back 19 times and dominate my thoughts in between. An American who would no longer feel at home anywhere but Reykjavík. Packed my bags, moved here, brought my kid, started a business and live happily ever after".

Mike Handley
Narrator and Anglicist (from the US)

Vital Links. *An aerial view of the central parts of Reykjavík. The equally important airport and old harbour as well as the old town are seen beyond the neighbouring town of Kópavogur (in the foreground). Mt. Akrafjall, Skarðsheiði and Esja are in the far background.*

the turfed farmhouses and cottages; most of them had only one or two storeys and were usually tarred on the outside.

In 1874, Iceland received its first, limited constitution from the Danish crown. At that time the population of Reykjavík was just over 2,000. One year later the Alþingi was given limited legislative powers and six years after that a new parliament building was constructed from blocks of Reykjavík lava. In 1904, when Iceland received partial home rule, the first Icelandic cabinet was formed. The Reykjavík population had now increased to 6,000. In 1918 Iceland was granted full home rule and the population was about 15,000.

The Old City Centre – Kvos. *Old and new meet in Reykjavík, notably in the city centre where old buildings like the Falcon House (in the background) blend in with newer buildings.*

At the end of the nineteenth century and up to the First World War, the town centre grew quite rapidly. A large number of attractive timber houses were erected in all shapes and sizes, some of them three or four storeys high. The style of the new buildings mainly derived from Denmark and Norway with carvings on the gables, small towers and large casement windows. Special buildings for stores and institutions also appeared. Unfortunately, however, much of this interesting architecture was destroyed in a fire that swept through the middle of town in 1915.

The first non-timber buildings at this time were mostly constructed from blocks of stone like the Alþingishús. A number of them were small, one-storey houses built mainly from stone but with some timber. Concrete dates back to the end of the nineteenth century, but was not used extensively for building in Iceland until the first two decades of the twentieth century. It was also during these years that the now colourfully painted corrugated iron that characterises so many Reykjavík timber houses became fashionable.

From the time that Reykjavík became an official municipality to 1912, all the roads and streets were dirt or gravel tracks which made commuting difficult whenever it rained or snowed heavily. Over the following decade, the town authorities laid them all with asphalt, or in some cases concrete, and today the road systems of the new suburbs are completed before the houses are erected.

Large concrete buildings and various schools and institutions, were built in the second and third decades of the twentieth century, and many of them in a style influenced by mainstream European architecture from 1850-1930. It is also at this time that Reykjavík's first leading architect, Guðjón Samúelsson, began to set his mark on the city. He and a few other architects and master builders were given the task of redesigning and supervising much of Reykjavík's new housing from this period until the early 1950s. More than any of his predecessors, Guðjón Samúelsson tried to develop a national style of architecture, which can be seen for example in the National Theatre building.

"Reykjavík becomes a better city to live in day by day. It gets better the more EVERYONE has access to go anywhere. The city also becomes cleaner every year. That's good but I miss the untouched beaches of old. However, the walking paths are a substitute!"
Guðmundur Magnússon, Actor/Manager of Day Care Centre for the Disabled

The Annual Night of Culture. *Reykjavíkians, as well as numerous visitors, gather in the city centre one evening in late August for education, entertainment, food and drink through the night.*

Hallgrímskirkja and Leifur Eiríksson. *The largest church in Reykjavík is named after the 17th century poet and ecclesiastical scholar, Hallgrímur Pétursson. The statue of Icelander Leifur Eiríksson (Leif Eriksson) is a gift from the people of the United States to commemorate the European discovery of North America, 500 years before Columbus visited.*

Kringlan. *A large cluster of high and low-profile buildings forms a new commercial centre. Its modern and bustling Kringlan Mall houses scores of stores and shops. Other large shopping centres are popping up, such as those in the neighbouring town of Kópavogur.*

From 1900-1935 a great portion of the town was built between two of the main roads at the time, Hringbraut and Snorrabraut. These comprised corrugated iron-covered timber or concrete houses which were relatively similar in style. The first apartment buildings also date from this period, almost all of them made of concrete. The town's main shopping area on Laugavegur, the lower part of Skólavörðustígur and Kvos began to take shape, rapidly taking the place of many of the small turf and timber houses and cottages in those areas. In the late 1930's Reykjavík's population had increased to 30,000.

A period of variety

From 1930 to 1950 various outlying areas of the town were developed, and a new style of architecture was evident in these the first of Reykjavík's suburbs, which mainly consisted of three to five storey apartment buildings. The Reykjavík airport, built by the British in 1940-1941, defined the limits of the town in that direction. Beside the airport, the British and then the Americans raised a number of other buildings necessary for their military activities, some of which are still standing.

For a very long time, Reykjavík was far from colourful to look at. One would have seen the occasional white house or building, but most of them were either brown or grey. However, after the last war, it became increasingly common for people to paint both the walls and the roofs of their houses in all kinds of colours. From 1950 to 1960 the town grew in size and stretched out in the direction of the Elliðaár river. The concrete and timber houses of the period were low, square buildings with flat roofs, a style that had never been seen before in Reykjavík. Both industrial and service areas began to spring up and again the town changed face rapidly. By 1965 the population was 75,000.

Over the following two decades, the town grew even more quickly, now expanding to the east of the Elliðaár river and north along the coast. Concrete was still the most important building material, but there was also an increase in the use of other materials such as aluminium, plastic, steel and glass. More and more Icelanders went abroad to study architecture and before too long Reykjavík began to look like a thoroughly modern city. The influences they brought back home were manifold, coming from countries and cultures as diverse as Scandinavia, the USA, Mexico, central Europe and the former eastern block.

The Pearl. *Underneath the huge steel and glass dome of the Pearl a part of the floor revolves – making the Pearl Restaurant a popular sightseeing panoramic vantage point.*

Reykjavík's characteristics

Various concepts concerning how the centre of town was to be modernised and an overall desire to maintain the pace of development met with little resistance. At that stage there were no properly formulated ideas about the preservation of Reykjavík's recent or more distant past and the result was that many of the houses and other build-

Árbær; the Reykjavík City Museum. *Guests flock to the Reykjavík City Museum where they can study the old houses, their interiors, utensils and toys. They can also, for example, see bygone workmanship or farm work in progress. The staff commonly dresses up in traditional clothing, such as peysuföt or upphlutur.*

ings in the older part of town were simply demolished. In some instances, large concrete buildings were erected in among the older timber houses, especially in the downtown area known as Kvos, and the general appearance of the centre of town was, and to some extent still is, both random and eclectic. Now there are clearer regulations concerning both the protection and preservation of older buildings and the construction of new buildings, and this has considerably improved the situation.

The Reykjavík Museum was founded in 1954. It became a partly outdoor museum in 1957. Its present site is at Árbær, on what was formerly a timber and turf farm close to the Elliðaár river. It is to this location that the town has moved some of its historic older buildings and a nineteenth century turfed church. The collection of houses at the Árbær Museum is not large, but it gives a very clear idea of Reykjavík's past. All the buildings there have been both renovated and preserved, and most of them contain furniture and other items from the period in which they were built. A great deal of effort has gone into creating the atmosphere of past times, allowing visitors to learn in an interesting first-hand manner more about the history of the town. The Museum is also in charge of all historical and archaeological matters in the Reykjavík.

One of the primary characteristics of Reykjavík is its size in relation to the number of its inhabitants; it is spread over a large area but is mainly composed of low buildings. Many of the more recent suburbs, especially those that have been built in the last three to four decades, have a homogenous style of architecture and a more open and spacious environment. Others show more internal variation with a multiplicity of styles and types of building. Yet none of these styles are peculiar to Reykjavík as such and the only buildings that are unusual in that sense are those built during what might be called the nationalist period of architecture from 1920-1950 and the colourful corrugated-iron clad timber houses.

The work of Guðjón Samúlesson, mentioned above, is striking in this respect. In many instances he drew inspiration from the old turf farmhouses and volcanic and basalt columns, and reworked those concepts in concrete. He is also known for adding various kinds of coverings for outer stone walls in order to make them look more as if they were part of the natural environment. This method, known as 'stoning' in Icelandic involved covering the walls with a coat of crushed rock.

There are almost no turf-roofed houses left in the city. On the other hand, there are quite a number of buildings with either interiors or exteriors made from Icelandic rock, such gabbro and rhyolite and, in some instances, large blocks of lava. For a period, Icelanders used compressed blocks of pumice for both building and covering walls but that practice has since disappeared. A recent interesting development has been the building of long exterior walls from native rock using either lava blocks or basalt boulders.. Corrugated iron, used for over a hundred years is still popular, mostly as roofing but occasionally also for walls and often in combination with other materials. Pre-dyed steel and aluminium have also come into use and add some variety. A few public buildings have aroused foreign interest for their unusual design, such as the Reykjavík City Hall, the National Library and the Supreme Court.

Laugavegur. The main shopping street in the old city centre is usually bustling with life. Many buildings on Laugavegur date from the period of the classic timber and concrete houses.

Corrugated Iron and Colour Displays *(Fríkirkjuvegur). Most people consider the old timber houses clad with painted corrugated iron and the general use of vivid colours to be one of the pre-eminent characteristics of Reykjavík.*

Air

"Visual Feminism"

Ragnheiður Jónsdóttir

The above phrase was first applied to many of the works of **Ragnheiður Jónsdóttir** by art historian Hannes Sigurðsson at a recent seminar on the life and works of the artist. The term "feminist surrealism" has also been used to describe her style.

Ragnheiður Jónsdóttir (b.1933) is well-known in Iceland for many decades of work, especially in the area of lithography, copper etching and drawing. She originally comes from rural south Iceland but moved to Reykjavík with her parents in 1953. After studying art in Reykjavík, Copenhagen and París, she began to work as a professional artist while also running a home and bringing up five sons. She describes herself as having been in a kind of ivory tower during that period, where she could create in private and look out at the world at the same time. She has lived in Garðabær for many years, working full time on her art. Beginning with etchings, she then turned her attention predominantly, in later years, to charcoal drawing. In 1993, she was officially invited to live and work in Sveaborg, Sweden.

Ragnheiður often creates works in series, comprising powerful and provocative, sometimes even threatening shapes and drawings. A few examples of her best known series would be her 'living' dresses, open books with pubic hair, a series of truly terrifying symbolic pictures illustrating the first five years of the new millennium, illustrations from the ancient Icelandic mystical poem, *Völuspá*, and large scale charcoal drawings of clouds and close-up aerial views of land or soil. "Solidarity with humankind and a strong sense of justice are the major themes of all she has produced," wrote Hjálmar Sveinsson, (Lífæðar, 1999, art.is.).

Ragnheiður Jónsdóttir has taken part in dozens of exhibitions, many of them solo. She has won a number of important prizes in the international arena, for example at Crackow, Frechen and Fredrikstad.

Ragnheiður is considered to be one of Iceland's most important artists in the areas of lithography, etching and drawing.

Hrímtjöld I (charcoal on paper, 150 x 150 cm, 1998) is from a series of ephemeral charcoal drawings that have semi-transparent quality and which portray both scenes of cold tranquillity and wintry turbulence. This abstract work evinces a strong interpretation of the natural elements and an equally strong influence from feminism.

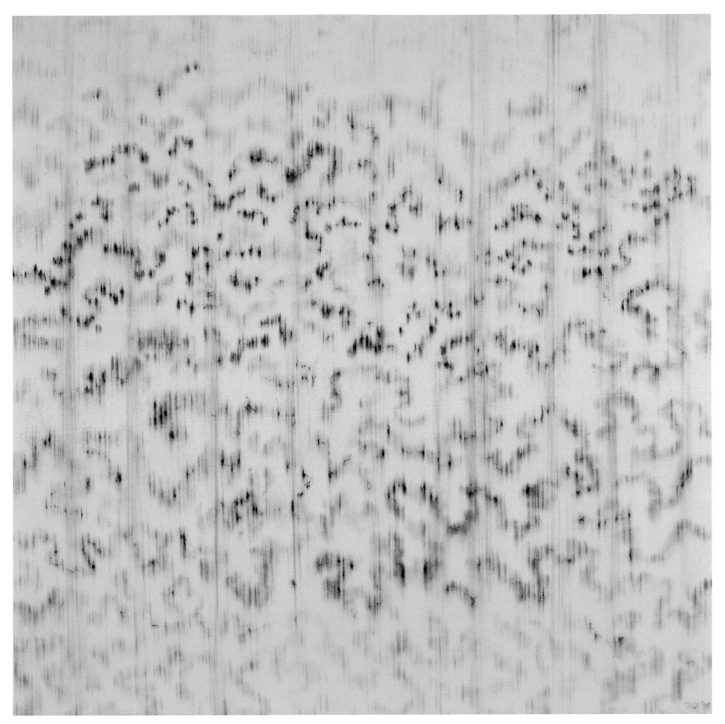

Hrímtjöld I.

A city for all seasons

An atlas will show you that Reykjavík is situated close to where 64° latitude bisects 22° longitude. That makes it the most northerly and most westerly capital in Europe; the next on both counts being Dublin some 1,550 km to the south-east. It will also be noticed that the 64th parallel runs through the centre of Norway, Sweden and Finland to the east, and close to Nuuk, the capital of Greenland and Iqaluit on Baffin Island in Nunavat, Canada to the west. If the climatic conditions of these places are compared to those of Iceland, it will be clear what part is played both by the ocean and by the size of the adjoining land masses. During the winter months, the average temperatures in those larger countries to the east and west of Iceland are usually much cooler than here. At the 64° latitude in Sweden, the temperature drops below – 20°C for long periods of time, and in Iqaluit, which is on the coast and usually flanked by floating ice, winter temperatures are between -20° to -30°C. By contrast, the average temperature in Reykjavík for January is about zero, although the lowest recorded temperature for the town was measured in 1918 at -24.5°C.

Average summer temperatures at similar latitudes in Scandinavia and mainland Canada tell a different tale, the norm in both places being +20°C, while Iqaluit and Nuuk are much cooler. Reykjavík is also rather cooler during the summer months, the average temperature for July being about 11°C. The highest recorded temperature for that month is 24.3°C (1976), but a typical Reykjavík 'heat wave' is somewhere between 14-18°C and lasts for just a few days at a time. Such calm sunny spells are quite rare, but can appear during spring, summer or autumn and are much appreciated by the locals. One of the reasons Reykjavík's climate is more moderate than that of places at a similar latitude is that the entire country is surrounded by the Gulf Stream that moves up through the Atlantic from the Caribbean.

Traffic Problems – Not Unknown. *Snow sometimes makes Reykjavík traffic slow or even brings it to a standstill. Slippery road conditions are common because of rapid shifts between frost and thaw.*

Lively conditions

While the climate in Reykjavík, then, is generally rather warm in winter and cool during summer for its latitude, it is also subject to abrupt change. Iceland lies in the main path of various low pressure systems coming from the south-west at what is known as the polar front. This means that the wind usually blows from three separate directions in succession whenever one of those low pressure systems moves over or close to the southern part of the country. First, a sharp south-easterly wind will arrive carrying some precipitation, usually to the south side of the island. That generally lasts for a few hours but can remain for up to at least twenty four hours. It is then followed by a rather short-lived sharp south-westerly with showers and, finally by a stiff northerly wind. Then the cloud cover begins to break up in the south part of the country and the sun will usually make a brief but welcome appearance. The mean annual precipitation for Reykjavík is about 900 mm while the Bláfjöll Mountains, some 500-700 m above sea level and only 20-25 km from the coast, are subject to 3,000 mm.

A Young Worker. *Rain or shine, active children always find something to do in their home garden.*

The Annual Night of Culture. *Grown-ups and children enjoy the splendid and colourful programme of activities, not to mention the colourful congregation of people.*

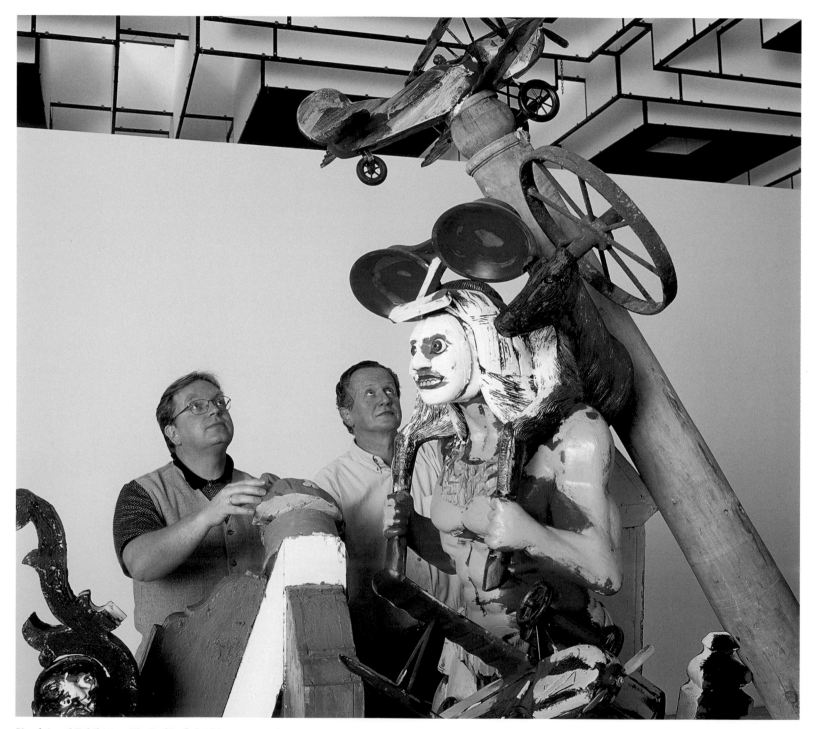

Karel Appel Exhibition. *The Reykjavík Art Museum organizes many art events every year. A large exhibition of the work of the Dutchman Karel Appel attracted a crowd in the summer 1999. Here, the director and museum manager busy themselves with its preparation .*

A Display of Ice Sculptures. *Artists carve sculptures from ice during the Annual Night of Culture.*

The Bunny Kids. *Companion and other domestic animals are common in Reykjavík. Horses, dogs and cats are the most numerous – but imported species such as hamsters and rabbits are also popular.*

A Sunny Day in Reykjavík. *Icelanders originally descended from Norway and the northern parts of Britain. Today however, they also have Danish and western European blood running in their veins.*

The best weather occurs just after a low pressure area moves away or passes over the ocean well off the south coast. Slow northerly winds and the dry, warm easterlies also make for pleasant weather in the capital, and when a low pressure area moves across the Atlantic far enough to the south of the country the weather is often warm and misty. Also, gentle southerly winds usually mean the weather is going to be mild and dry. Continual fluctuations between periods of frost and thaw characterise Reykjavík and add to the variation, and it is not uncommon during the winter months for snow to fall in the morning and be replaced by rain in the afternoon.

A few times each winter, Reykjavík will be subject to heavy blizzards, making road travel in town difficult. The roads and other forms of communication out to the rest of the country are almost impossible. But even when there is no snow, low pressure areas from October to April can often be very deep and the cause of heavy rainstorms and serious gales. Deep low pressure areas over the east part of the country or high pressure over Greenland, on the other hand, result in a ferocious and blustery north wind that keeps the temperature in Reykjavík down at -5° to -10°, exacerbated by a heavy wind chill factor.

Yet whatever happens, the weather conditions in Reykjavík have a variety and variability that seldom make life boring. Thus the weather also makes constant demands on one's patience and often requires one to be extremely cautious when road conditions are at their worst. By contrast, the weather in Reykjavík during the winter can also be pleasantly cool and sunny, and when a slow south-westerly constantly shifts the clouds, the quality of the daylight and the dancing of the sun's rays make an enchanting sight.

The joys of spring

Spring – by which is meant in these climes, the time when the grass begins to turn green again and there are no visible signs of overnight frost – does not usually arrive in Reykjavík until the middle of April and continues to the end of May or, in a cold year, early June. That is not to say, however, that such pleasant conditions are here to stay. At various times during the spring, the weather may worsen and either grow very cold or result in snow. The people of Reykjavík tend not to pay too much attention to such 'relapses.' Indeed, they are often over-optimistic about the weather in late spring and rather too hasty to put on their summer clothes. By the end of March, the days and nights become equally long, and then the nights begin to recede until, in early June. Soon afterwards, grass, at first more yellow than green, appears from under the melting ice in the public parks and private gardens and the trees begin to shake off their winter apparel. Over a period of three to four weeks, the entire Reykjavík environment changes from grey or brown to green. Traditionally, the radio announces the arrival of the first migrating bird, the golden plover and the arctic tern. Children and adults celebrate the coming of summer each year, according to the ancient seasonal calendar, with a parade in late April on a common holiday.

Scouts and Students on Independence Day. *The placing of a wreath at the memorial statue of 19th century leader Jón Sigurðsson is an integral part of the festivities every 17th of June.*

Independence Day – The National Holiday, June 17. *Since 1944, this particular day continues to draw large and patriotic crowds to the city centre.*

A Day for Children and a Bright Future. *On June 17, children... and more children may be the most conspicuous aspect of Independence Day celebrations.*

People begin to tend to their gardens and fix whatever damage the winter has done to their houses. And when school is out at the end of May, a large proportion of the town's teenagers are employed by City Hall in cleaning up the streets, public parks and gardens. By the time Iceland's national independence day arrives on June 17, the city is brimming with activity. Thousands of people flock to the centre of town to join in the celebrations which last all day and often through to the early hours of the morning. The celebrations begin by honouring the memory of Jón Sigurðsson who led the Icelandic struggle for independence. That struggle ended with the official establishment of Iceland as an independent democracy on June 17, 1944. The celebrations are followed by large open-air festivities in the middle of town.

Eternal summer

Fish for Sale in the Western Part of Reykjavík.
Once, most sea fishing was done from small boats. Some still is and many small boats are kept in the old harbour. Some of the fishermen continue to use the western coastline and pull boats ashore in the traditional way (north of the airport).

The summer in Reykjavík lasts from the beginning of June to the middle of August. On June 23, Midsummer's Day, the sun sinks just below the horizon for one to two hours but its rays keep the sky bright. From various heights and along the north coast of the city, when the weather is fine one can see the red sun hovering above the Snæfellsnes glacier, shedding purple and pink light across the northern sky. It is on days like this that Icelanders seem unusually susceptible to talk of fairies and folklore.

For most of the summer, there is daylight for fourteen to twenty two hours, and for long periods the moon and the stars only appear for a very short time or are completely invisible. The brightness of the air has an almost inebriating effect. People stay awake longer, dress up in fashionable clothes no matter how warm or cold the weather, and try to spend as much time in the open air as possible. The streets, parks, coffee houses, leisure centres and swimming pools are filled with people. The sports and leisure centre at Laugardalur has a number of different activities to offer, including a large pool and health club, a gymnasium, public gardens, a family amusement park and a small zoo. On a good summer's day, Laugardalur is teeming with people, and the same may be said of all the walking, jogging, cycling and roller-skating paths scattered around the town. Bird-life on Tjörnin (city lake) is also a popular attraction, as is the old harbour.

Anglers make their way to the Elliðaár river, where the fishing season is officially opened each year by the mayor, who is traditionally the first to

"As you return home from the large cities abroad – where you may wander for days without coming across anything but walls on all sides, asphalt beneath your feet and a grey sky above – you feel how good it is to live and move about in a city that holds the vastness of the world: mountains on one side, an endless ocean on the other – and the big sky above. You feel that you can get here or leave anytime because planes are constantly airborne or landing at the airport, which is like the eye of the city and a heavenly ladder".

Einar Kárason, Writer

The Golfer and the Eider Duck. *Reykjavík and its neighbouring towns offer numerous golf courses to golfing enthusiasts. And enthusiasts they are because nesting eider ducks and Arctic terns don't distract them. The birds are enthusiastic, too, because they don't give an inch of their territory away to the players.*

Kolaportið ("The Coal Yard"). *The Reykjavík Flea Market is quite popular. And so is the "national dish": a hot dog with various condiments called "ein með öllu" – or "one with everything on it".*

So Light, So light... *A participant in one of Reykjavík's many outdoor festivities salutes the air.*

attempt to catch a salmon. Others prefer to fish for trout in nearby lakes and rivers. Since the city also has a large area reserved for stables, thousands of individuals take advantage of the good weather to go horseback riding and can be seen all over the outskirts of town. It is even possible to play a midnight round of golf in Reykjavík.

The people of Reykjavík are also avid sunbathers, lying out in their gardens or indeed any grassy plot in order to obtain a tan. In fact, sunbathing is so common that some visitors might think they were a great deal further south than Iceland. By late evening, town begins to fill again, and one can see people wandering between the many clubs, discos, bars, coffee houses and restaurants of downtown.

But the weather is not always bright. Anyone living in Reykjavík during the summer must learn to expect heavy showers and cold spells that make it feel like winter has arrived prematurely. Fortunately, it only takes one good day in most people's minds to dispel all thoughts of cold or rain, and one recent international survey revealed Icelanders to be the most optimistic nations in the world.

Dozens of Cafés and Restaurants. *Many and varied pubs, cafés and restaurants dot the old city centre. In the evenings, especially on weekends, most of them have no dearth of customers.*

Autumn chills

The first signs of autumn are overnight frost and frozen dew and are usually experienced in late August. The days begin to shorten, the moon reappears in the sky and the berries are beginning to ripen on the heaths. Just as in spring, and especially in the month of May, late August and September is a time when the weather is calm and still. The leaves on the city's many deciduous trees begin to fade and fall while the pines and firs ensure that there is still some greenery. Both in and around the city, especially at Heiðmörk, one can see what Icelanders refer to as the 'autumn colours': soft shades of light green, yellow, brown and purple, a delicate symphony of tones that make autumn a welcome season.

The last cruise ships dock in the Reykjavík harbour and suddenly most of the foreign guests and visitors disappear from the streets of town like migrating birds. Many tourists have yet to discover the joys of an Icelandic autumn.

The city's inhabitants, like most Icelanders, tend to become strangely energised by the autumn season, and have transferred their attention over the past few decades from simply fishing and farming into a much greater variety of occupations. Life in Reykjavík during these months seems to consist of finding some intensely interesting new activity, a tendency that is apparent in schools,

"I like to live in Reykjavík, aside from the traffic. Too many Icelanders don't know how to drive. I live in the suburbs and I find that good for my kids. My work is good. I drive in shifts and that suits me fine for the time being".

Sædís Samúelsdóttir, Bus Driver

A Bookshop. *It's said that, per capita, nowhere are so many books published, so many books bought and so much discussed about literature as in Iceland.*

In the Heart of Reykjavík. *Christmas is important in Iceland. The nation's largest municipality brims with life and its main business areas are very busy. Some people only go "to see and be seen".*

The Elusive and Tingling Air of Christmas. *An air only understood by those experiencing the last days before Christmas reigns in the main streets of the old city centre. Thousands upon thousands find their way into shops, cafés and restaurants on December 23.*

businesses and shops. People seem to be more preoccupied than usual and the pace of life increases. Reykjavík is very much a city of cars despite the high standard of public transport. It has been estimated that, on any given day, there are now about 100,000 cars driving around Reykjavík. By comparison, there were only 700-800 in 1930. But despite the large and growing volume of traffic the air remains relatively clean and measurements reveal that the level of pollution is almost always very low. The reason for this is that the constant winds usually manage to clear the city air in a very short period of time.

In late October or early November the first snow usually begins to fall. It is at this time, one month after the autumn equinox, that the old-style calendars record the arrival of the first day of winter, but unlike the advent of summer, there is no corresponding celebration.

Moody winter

Autumn. Reykjavík is a city for all seasons, always fresh – and always interesting.

The Icelandic reference to the weather gods (plural) reflects the influence of the old Nordic religion. If they still exist these gods are even more temperamental and unpredictable in winter than at any other time of the year. By late November and early December, however, the chances of snow increase significantly and the temperature can stay well below zero for days on end. Such periods are usually interspersed with slightly warmer days, but never more than a few degrees above freezing point. Sometimes there is little snow before Christmas. In moderation, it is a welcome sight, especially since a light covering of snow reflects the light and makes the days a little brighter.

Just as elsewhere, the days and weeks leading up to Christmas are full of activity and not only in the shops and stores. Yet, the people of Reykjavík, like all Icelanders, appear to invest even more time and energy into Christmas celebrations than many of their neighbours. The reasons for this are various, partly religious and partly because the winter season is so long that Christmas presents itself as a celebration of lights. It is also, of course, the time when daylight slowly but surely begins to lengthen. Icelanders make the most of this, also celebrating Thorlak's Mass on December 23 with its own special range of foods and plentiful amounts of wine and spirits. Indeed, all through the second and third weeks of December, many companies, institutions and individuals gather together at what is known as a *jólaglögg* (lit. "Yuletide bright").

Reykjavík and its environs have an unusually large number of shops and

"The size of Reykjavík is pleasant. There's always something going on. You can always find things to do like going out in the evening or playing golf. Then, there are so many beautiful women in the city and nature is always close by – in any sense of the term. I'm from Ólafsvík and always look for fine landscape and unspoilt nature. You find it in Reykjavík".
Ómar Ingi Magnússon, Filling Station Attendant

Fireworks. *Twilight on a mid-winter afternoon. A cascade of fire with the settling Arctic sun in the background.*

Kringlan. *Reykjavík's first mall, seen here shortly before Christmas. Kringlan is situated in a new business area of the city, an area that also draws cultural institutions such as the Reykjavík City Theatre.*

New Year's Eve. *Reykjavik is undoubtedly the city for fireworks on New Year's Eve. To the surprise of many visitors, the show is not a municipal event. Instead, it's a synchronized midnight opus by every household in the city! Icelanders buy most of their fireworks from rescue teams and sports clubs, which use the profits to partly finance their activities.*

stores in proportion to the town's population. They range from small specialist shops to large-scale supermarkets and shopping centres. The largest of these is the mall known as Kringlan, which houses a large variety of stores and which is being expanded all the time. The main shopping street in downtown Reykjavík is Laugavegur, and despite the existence of the malls, it remains popular. One of the more interesting new features in town is the covered market of Kolaport, opposite the old harbour – a kind of flea market, food emporium and shopping centre rolled into one. During the week before Christmas all the shopping streets and malls stay open very late and there are all sorts of activities going on, including concerts, poetry recitals, book promotions, parties and parades. The custom of decorating the outsides of buildings with lights makes the Christmas season in Reykjavík quite special. Another tradition is the displaying of the 'advent' lights, candles or electric light bulbs set up in a small seven branched candelabra, in the windows of most households.

"The capital is a pretty good place to live in. Good fishing grounds aren't far away and the city's not too big. I've worked as a metal craftsman onshore for 30 years but I've got to get out to sea as often as I can – to fetch the breeze and be outdoors in the middle of nature".
Sigursteinn Hjaltested, Metal Craftsman and Seaman

Both December and January are quite dark months, the minimum daylight varying somewhere between 4 to 5 hours. After the Christmas celebrations, many people find this period of the year the most difficult to endure, but research into the depression that often settles indicates that it is not as widespread in Iceland as in places with a similar lack of winter daylight. The reasons for this are unknown.

Reykjavík is also one of the few cities in the world where one can see the northern lights or Aurora Borealis, otherwise a common phenomenon in all arctic regions. Actually, they are not a seasonal phenomenon at all but are constantly created when charged particles from the sun are attracted to the earth's magnetic field and drawn rapidly into our atmosphere. On arrival they collide with various gases, such as oxygen, and illuminate them. Although the northern lights can appear in many colours, the most common are green, purple and yellow, bending and swerving across the sky at a height of about 100 to 150 km. They can best be seen when the sky is very dark and cloudless, and are especially obvious on a still clear winter's night. Naturally, the streets of Reykjavík are very well lit during the winter and the northern lights are much more dazzling outside the built up areas. Ten to fifteen minutes drive from the outer suburbs will afford a spectacular view of them. So beautiful are they on occasion that one is almost persuaded to believe that the long winters are a small price to pay for being able to witness them in all their silent glory.

The City Lake in Winter. *Some duck species, greylag geese and whooper swans are the most prominent species during winter months. Ice-skaters are prominent here as well.*

A Sky Ablaze with Northern Lights. Looking across the city to the northwest, Reykjavík glitters with light. The sky above spills over with restless northern lights that show a different, even more beautiful display – this one of green and yellow shimmering lights. The phenomenon is akin to fluorescent light and commonly occurs about 100 km above the earth's surface.

In late winter, Icelanders hold a festival known as *þorrablót*. This is an ancient custom which has recently been taken up again and consists of eating traditional foods, often accompanied by vast amounts of alcohol. These foods include various kind of offal, smoked lamb, blood sausage etc. as well as dried fish, Icelandic flat bread, and naturally fermented shark meat. Much of this is what Icelanders call 'sour food,' i.e. meat that has been marinated in whey. Most restaurants in Reykjavík now offer this special cuisine and groups of people from the same workplace often meet at them to celebrate together. For those who are not fond of this seasonal food, it should be noted that Reykjavík's restaurants also offer a large number of foreign cuisines, including Thai, Indian, Mexican, Italian, amongst others. Failing that, there is always the hot dog stand and a host of other fast-food places.

"Komdu sæll". This greeting ("Come, be happy!") is often heard on the street. Reykjavík really is a small community compared to most other world capitals.

Culture needs breathing space

It has long since been proved that culture thrives best where it is given sufficient space – in other words where it is not constantly subject to rules, regulations and prejudice. In this respect, Iceland not only has enough actual space and a good atmosphere (in both senses of the word), but it is a place where culture, education and the arts are relatively free from restriction and there is a great deal of public interest in all three. They also receive good coverage in the media. Moreover, Icelanders are neither short of opinions nor shy about expressing them.

The capital has a number of multi-screen cinemas, two large theatres, (the National and City Theatres) as well as many smaller theatre companies. Some of the galleries are owned and run by the city or state, such as the National Gallery beside Tjörnin. But there are also a great many smaller, private galleries and studios scattered all over the city where artists create and sell their own work. Similarly, the number of musicians is considerable, engaged as they are in performing both classical and popular music, especially in pop groups. Add to these the jazz groups, the chamber music ensembles and the Icelandic Symphonic Orchestra and it will be apparent how much interest Icelanders show in creating, performing and listening to music. Opera in Reykjavík is performed at the Reykjavík Opera House which is situated downtown. There are a number of music schools in the city and The Icelandic Dance Ensemble is also situated here as well as other dance groups. Icelanders also appear to hold the world record in the number of films

"It's good to work in Reykjavík and it's a charming place to live in. Here I learned my trade. It proved to be a good choice. The city's best gift was my wife. We lived happily together for 54 years. Reykjavík is a great and clean city with adequate power supplies, hot water for good health-care and fine, soothing fresh water. The city's health institutions have improved and I've been enjoying life in one of them, an assisted living home for the elderly. I also enjoy participating in an organization for former Boy Scouts and in the Association for Blind People. Well, you could improve the bus system and the traffic – but so many things are wanted but not granted".

Þórður Jónsson, former Engine Master

A Fine, Stylish Motorway Overpass for Hikers and Cyclists. Its construction has brought international attention, including the front cover of the book New Architecture ELEVEN.

A Monologue in the Former City Theatre (Iðnó). *A few large – and many small – theatre companies operate in Reykjavík. Each produces a number of shows and performances and all are popular venues.*

Public, Poetic Reading. *A member of the younger generation of writers, Gerður Kristný, reads from her work during a literary evening shortly before Christmas.*

The National Gallery. A large collection of domestic and foreign artwork is kept in this elegant art museum. The profile of the elegant lady is by Picasso.

A City Dog. Dogs have been allowed in Reykjavík with some restrictions for a few years now.

seen per capita, and there is a very large selection of plays or shows at any given time. There are also dozens of weekly concerts and even more art exhibitions. The written word also has a very special place in Icelandic culture. Proud of their ancient sagas and eddic poetry, Icelanders are unusually fond of writing, reading and reciting their literature. There are many large publishers in town and plenty of bookstores, selling either new or second-hand books. Hundreds of books of all kinds are published each year, but reaches a peak in the last few weeks before Christmas when the media is inundated with advertisements, recitals and discussion programmes. Finally, the cultural exchange between Icelanders and other nations is evident from for example the Nordic House, which is designed by the architect Alvar Aalto.

Other forms of art, craft and design are too many to be numbered here, but gold- and silversmiths and potters seem to have multiplied of late and are enjoying a wave of public response. All in all, the amount of cultural activity in Reykjavík would easily be at home in a city twice its size.

Like other small nations, the capital serves as the centre for most further education. Most of the specialist schools and colleges can be found there as well as one of the two sites of the University of Iceland; the other is in Akureyri in the north. The University of Iceland, first established in 1911, currently serves about 6,000 students. If all the schools, from primary to university level as well as other similar educational institutions are counted, almost half the population of the city spends the day inside a classroom. The first elementary school in Reykjavík dates back to 1831. Reykjavík is also the centre of the country's health system and is therefore the home of the largest hospitals and medical research institutes. For many years the city ran its own hospital, but it has now been absorbed into the state medical service.

Museums and art

In addition to the Árbær museum, Reykjavík also contains a number of other cultural and art museums and collections. The City Library, for example, has branches in many of the suburbs as well as a travelling library service. The city also has a large documentary section and a photography museum, and City Hall takes an active part in exhibiting, promoting and supporting all areas of education and the arts.

The largest art museum owned and run by the city of Reykjavík is the Reykjavík Art Museum, housed in the specially designed building known as Kjarvalsstaðir on Miklatún. The building is named after Iceland's most highly regarded and honoured artist, Jóhannes S. Kjarval, and the gallery is the home of much of that artist's most important work. It also has regular exhibitions of both Icelandic and foreign artists and designers each year. In April 2000 the museum will also use a large part of the recently renovated Harbour House, down by the old docks. There it intends to open an art centre, based on a collection of works by the internationally acclaimed Icelandic artist known as Erró.

A Chamber Orchestra. *Many jazz or folk music bands, pop groups, classical music groups or orchestras perform in the capital. Here, a Reykjavík chamber orchestra is about to conclude a concert in the neighbouring town of Kópavogur's Music Hall. When it comes to culture, the six municipalities in the Greater Reykjavík area are more or less unified.*

Ballet. *The Icelandic Ballet Ensemble commonly performs at the Reykjavík City Theatre and has performed both classical and modern ballet.*

Government and commerce

THE ICELANDIC PHALLOLOGICAL MUSEUM

Reykjavík is the seat of Iceland's government. The Alþingi (the Icelandic Parliament), the various ministries and most other major public institutions are in the centre of town, as is the presidential office, though the official residence of the President of Iceland remains at Bessastaðir. All the political parties have their headquarters in Reykjavík, and the same is true of the major organised interest groups and consumer societies. Reykjavík City Hall is one of the nation's largest employers with a total staff of over 8,500 in 1999.

Vigdís Finnbogadóttir. *She is among only a handful of internationally known Icelandic contemporary personalities. Pop singer Björk would be another example.*

In the past, all municipal matters were handled by the 'landfógeti' or National Bailiff, the first man to hold that office being the already mentioned Skúli Magnússon. In 1803, a sheriff's office was also established and its first task was to deal with the first and only concerted attempt to seize power in the country. In 1809, a Danish adventurer, known as Jörundur the Dog-Day King, sailed to Iceland with a band of men, and with the assistance of some of the native people he managed to take control of Reykjavík, and therefore the whole country for several weeks. Reykjavík's first town council was appointed in 1836. In 1906, the first secret ballot was held for town council elections on a modern basis. In 1908, women won the right to vote in council elections for the first time and Reykjavík also had its first democratically elected mayor in the same year. Many of the departments and branches of City Hall were not gathered together into one place until 1992, when it moved to new premises overlooking Tjörnin.

Despite the spread of the industrial revolution in the eighteenth century, it effectively played little part in Reykjavík's development until the end of the nineteenth century. Fishing was mainly conducted from open sailing vessels or rowboats, which set out from bays and small harbours all around the capital's coastline. Most of the catch was worked as stock- or salt-fish. Commerce began to expand rapidly and was given an entirely free hand in 1855. From 1860-1870, fishing took another leap when schooners and large sailing boats replaced the traditional open boats. Reykjavík enjoyed the considerable profits of its fishing industry which increased again significantly in the first decade of the twentieth century when the first trawlers appeared. From then on, trawling, processing and fishing technology partly formed the basis of Reykjavík's and Iceland's economy.

"Even though I was born and bred in Akureyri, I felt that I was home when I settled in Reykjavík. My feeling may only portray the incredible human skill of adaptation but I already knew then that I would more or less live and work in the city for the rest of my life. Now, 35 years later, the city still fulfils its promises. I've mostly lived in the old part of town, married and had children, with my work at the National Theatre never far away. Sometimes, I've been so busy that my contact with the city has only been superficial: I'd walk across Laugavegur but not along it, and Tower Square never seemed to be still. It has been a privilege to live and work here".

Arnar Jónsson, Actor

Ásmundur Sveinsson Museum. *Reykjavík is a city of numerous galleries, workshops and museums. The late Ásmundur Sveinsson is one of the better-known Icelandic sculptors.*

Old Times. *Reminding everyone of bygone days, fishermen and their small fishing boats still linger in Reykjavík.*

New Times. *Complicated and time-consuming genetic research is at the forefront of the Icelandic scientific community. The Reykjavík-based company DeCode has garnered widespread international attention.*

Reykjavík City Hall. *The building was constructed alongside the city lake and is regarded as one of the more interesting large buildings in Reykjavík from the late 20th century.*

Two Different Ways of Going to Work. More than 100,000 private cars and city buses roam the Reykjavík streets.

President Ólafur Ragnar Grímsson. Traditionally, decorated photographs of current Presidents are kept on display in shop windows on Independence Day, June 17.

The Police. *Iceland's unarmed police only have roots back to the middle of the 19th century.*

From 1908, there have been council elections in Reykjavík every four years and nearly twenty individuals have held the office of mayor, two of them women. In many cases, the mayor has moved on to the national arena of politics, often ending at the head of government as prime minister. Currently the governing body of the city council comprises fifteen representatives in addition to the mayor, and presides directly over a large number of sub-committees.

An environmentally friendly capital

Reykjavík aims at becoming the most environmentally friendly capital in the north, in conjunction with the 1992 agreement formulated by the UN concerning the environment and development (Agenda 21). This agreement is based on the concept of sustainable development or, in other words, a policy that will help to enrich the quality of life without over-exploiting nature. In the light of this agreement Reykjavík became a member of the Aalborg Convention (an extension of Agenda 21) signed by a host of European city and town councils officially committed to sustainable development. These councils endorsed a framework plan known as Local Agenda 21, which allows each of them to put the central concept into effect in a way that best suits individual conditions. Each council will therefore set up its own programme for environmental issues, placing special emphasis on a number of factors such as education and the full participation of the inhabitants in any given area. This plan will be the basis of transforming Reykjavík into a town that pays permanent attention to renewing its natural resources. One of the latest developments in this plan is the co-operation of numerous different companies (SKIL 21), working collectively to categorise all their waste products and then utilising whatever is organic for the cultivation of grass and trees within the area said to have been originally claimed by the first settler of Iceland, Ingólfur Arnarson.

The Reykjavík Marathon. *Every August, Icelandic and foreign marathon runners compete along the capital's streets.*

Reykjavík City Centre and the Old Town. *To the left, this aerial view reveals the western part of the old town (Vesturbær). Tjörnin (the lake) is in the middle, with the original city centre (Kvos) behind the lake including numerous official buildings. To the right, the eastern part of the old town (Austurbær) covers a small hill.*

Water

"From words to objects, and back again "

Kristinn E. Hrafnsson

This is the way in which the artist **Kristinn E. Hrafnsson** describes one of his approaches to his work. Philosophical reflections concerning the meanings of words, objects and places have been the inspiration of much of his creative activity and constitute its main themes. Kristinn draws the conceptual meanings of words towards objects and vice versa. He has remarked that he is trying to "create places with objects that have either a very clearly defined meaning, or a wholly undefined meaning other than simply existing."

Kristinn E. Hrafnsson (b. 1960) studied art at Akureyri, Reykjavík and Munich. He has taken part in over thirty joint exhibitions and held nine solo exhibitions. He has also won numerous honours and awards.

Both Kristinn's work and the materials he uses show great variety. His sculptures, whether in stone, metal or wood, are commonly supplemented by inscriptions of various kinds. He also uses found objects in his work where he finds them appropriate. Many of his works are intended as a part of the environment to decorate, to provoke thought or as a memorial to the times in which we live. Kristinn has shown consistent interest in community planning and what part it plays in the interface between art and the environment.

His combination of a highly disciplined but fully imaginative approach to his work has drawn the particular attention of critics.

*The work **Það sem eftir er** (rhyolite, 20 x 30 x 100 cm) dates from 1998. The artist says that it is about time and that it should therefore be able to "manage to be an historical site, a landmark, a solemn oath, and/or their tombstone at the same time. More than anything else, it is about the time we choose these things as well as being a work of art. The title (lit. 'what is left') denotes how it sinks into the marshland and becomes part of them, just like all we create."*

Það sem eftir er.

Everything moves on

Of the so-called four basic elements that ancient societies believed made up the world, earth, fire, air and water, the last has the most unique characteristics. It has often been remarked that "everything moves on," an adage that links the essential nature of water with a process of never-ending change.

Water is made up of two of the most common gases in our atmosphere, oxygen and hydrogen, and as everyone knows it is tasteless and colourless in its purest form. It can be found deep below the ground as well as on the surface and in the atmosphere and, unlike almost all other substances it expands on cooling. Water, then, is perhaps the essence of life, for not only are all creatures dependent on it, it also constitutes most of their being. That includes man, who uses and relies on water for almost everything he does.

The people of Reykjavík have plenty of water, not only in the surrounding sea but also in the many streams and lakes in the area. Moreover, the fresh water used for domestic consumption is not only Reykjavík's but the whole country's most precious resource. In addition, water in all its forms plays an important role in the shaping of the landscape.

Reynisvatn. There are plenty of fishing opportunities in the Greater Reykjavík area.

From the mountains to the faucet

In many parts of the country, the bedrock is unusually hot. Fortunately, however, the upper 100-300 metres of rock and soil strata are by contrast quite cold. Annual fluctuations in the air temperature have very little effect at all. At a depth of 10-100 meters the average temperature in most parts of Iceland is somewhere between 2-10°C. On the other hand, the total annual precipitation amounts to billions of tons. Some of that water sinks only a short distance through the surface towards the bedrock and then runs along fissures and cracks until it reaches the sea. It is this cold groundwater that comprises much of Iceland's cold water supply. The remainder can be found in the lakes and glaciers.

The cold groundwater in Iceland is one of the best available anywhere in the world. As either rain or melted snow, it already contains both chlorine and carbon dioxide in very small quantities. As it sinks into and moves through the rock, it gathers various other substances. Much of the rock is one form of basalt or another, either lava, palagonite or sediments. These substances give the water an acceptable acidic level and increase its quality. The groundwater travels most readily through the bedrock formed in recent eruptions and through the lava since both are full of fissures and cracks. And indeed, that is how it flows in the Reykjavík area. For example, one such area stretches from the Elliðaár river to the Bláfjöll mountains and is now Reykjavík's largest reservoir. That water has fallen as precipitation on the northern flank of the Bláfjöll range and sunk through the lava and

The Outer Harbour. *The streets Sætún and Skúlagata form a continuous seaside "boulevard" with a walkers' pathway. The view is good across the small fjord of Kollafjörður and on to Mt. Esja.*

The Outer Harbour. *Since the earliest of times after the settlement of Reykjavík, large ships have always anchored in the small bay southeast of the old harbour. The Queen Elizabeth is one of the largest ships ever to call.*

The Lake and Fríkirkjan Church. *People like to stroll along the banks, take breaks and eye the scenery including the bird life. The Hljómskálagarðurinn park is in the background.*

palagonite in the uninhabited area some 10-20 km from the city, whence it makes its way forward to the margin of the lava fields in Heiðmörk.

The harnessing of water resources in Reykjavík has a long history. To begin with there were just a few wells within the borders of the town. The first of these, no longer in use, and which dates back to the time the area was first settled, is still visible in Aðalstræti, where a pump from the nineteenth century marks the spot. As Reykjavík grew into a village and then a town, the number of wells increased and by the beginning of the twentieth century there were about thirty of them. At the same time there were no pipes that fed water into the houses nor any drainage system to dispense with waste water. For a long time, people were actually employed as water carriers, by all accounts a difficult and unhygienic occupation. Many people, though, fetched their own water and the main water posts thus became the town's main meeting places for news and gossip. Washing clothes required less water and many women had to take their family's clothes and linen all the way to the hot springs at Laugardalur, Reykjavík's traditional washing place for centuries on end.

"I was born in the outskirts of Reykjavík and brought up in the "rural" parts of the city, a true privilege. The fields and coastline at Laugarnes were my playgrounds. There I learned to read nature: the flowers, the birds...and life as it really is. I even started my working career there. Now, no longer an outlying part of town, Laugarnes still exists and is still a site where nature shines, like Heiðmörk and Elliðaár. They are all unique in a city, a city that also holds the arts and culture to an international standard. I truly enjoy all this, especially since all the city's different worlds exist within the distance of a few kilometres".

Þuríður Sigurðardóttir , singer, stewardess and art student

Fyssa *("Falling water", by Rúrí). Outdoor sculptures and statues are unusually common in Reykjavík. They display a broad range of styles and artistic periods – from reproductions of Greek statues to classic works by Icelandic sculptors like Einar Jónsson – and to new works such as this one.*

Reykjavík's Main Fountain. *The city needs about 50,000 tons of fresh water every 24 hours. Some of it gushes from the only large fountain in the city, in the south part of Tjörnin.*

In 1906 Reykjavík was subject to a serious epidemic, probably the result of using polluted water. At about the same time, it became clear that the town was also suffering from a general shortage of water. It therefore suddenly became crucial to improve the hygiene of the watering places and ensure that everybody had access to enough clean water. This soon led to the development of an underground piped water system, the first section of which was laid from the Elliðaár river. This system was brought into use in June 1909, but was regarded at the time as only a temporary measure. Soon afterwards, the town's water supplies were supplemented with water from natural springs known as the Gvendarbrunnar springs at the edge of the Heiðmörk lava. The main water system was connected up to that area in October 1909.

Reykjavík had found a viable solution to its immediate water crisis and now benefited from access to abundant supplies of fresh clean water. Inevitably, once the system was put into use, the demand for water multiplied quickly over a very short period, from 18 to 180 litres a day for each inhabitant. The town therefore had no choice but to lay a proper freshwater and drainage system almost immediately.

Ice and Water. Iceland is rich in first-class fresh drinking water.

Water's Underworld

The Reykjavík Water Works has been in charge of supplying the city's water for almost a century and has since gradually expanded the distribution system in accordance with the city's growth. It also serves the fresh water needs of the neighbouring towns of Kópavogur, Seltjarnarnes and Mosfellsbær.

The open wells at Gvendarbrunnar proved sufficient for Reykjavík's purposes for a long time, but inevitably the time arrived when the city's waterworks had not only to investigate other possible supplies but to take further measures to ensure that they met the desirable standards of hygiene. In 1978, shallow wells were sunk at the edge of the lava close to Gvendarbrunnar and later on to the south of the same spot. Beside the bore holes there were smaller closed wells sunk into the edge of the lava. This was effected by creating a large underground station to contain some wells, pumps and a central control system for the entire supply. It is by any standards a very impressive construction which looks more like a secret underground research plant from a science fiction tale than a water supply unit. The interior walls of the subterranean caves are bare lava rock and the plant contains a small but interesting museum.

"It's a rare privilege – or an unbelievably lucky fate, in both space and time – to work in this place, of all places on earth – to be granted the status of being an Icelander – especially nowadays – and to participate in the consolidation of this young society where so many things are left to do, the opportunities so plentiful and the human problems so small – when one compares Iceland to most other societies in our times! Reykjavík, small as it is, is a true capital city in international terms. It reflects and fits the mould of a humane and good society – but is willing to do even better".
Vilhjálmur Lúðvíksson, Chemical Engineer and Director of RANNÍS

Reykjavík and Clean Hydropower. *Seen here is one of the older of the hydropower plants that supply Reykjavík. This one is on the Sog river, some 70 km east of Reykjavík.*

The Water Work Caverns. *A large part of the control unit plus some of the water wells of the Reykjavík Water Works are located in a man-made lava cavern, a short distance east of the city.*

A High-tech Fish Factory. *Fishing, fishing technology, fish processing and fish export provide Iceland with 60-70% of its export income.*

Home with the Catch. *A large proportion of the catch is processed at sea and then delivered by the fishing vessel to the nearest port or its home port. Reykjavík has a strong fishing industry.*

The total number of wells serving Reykjavík and its environs has increased in recent years and deep wells sunk in nearby areas have now become important parts of the system. Currently water is pumped from about twenty separate wells into a two million litre reservoir beside the water sources. From there it runs along two main pipelines to the distribution centre in the city. This distribution system uses five storage tanks, 30 main pumping stations and over 500 km pipelines.

Sufficient Supplies for Two Million

It is estimated that the average Reykjavík family uses about 880 litres of cold water per day, or about 220 litres per capita for the same period of time. Most of that water (45%) runs literally straight down the toilet but a large proportion of it also goes to serve the needs of industry and various services. The total amount used for domestic use is therefore about 15,000,000 litres (15,000 tons) per day while companies and institutions use about 35,000,000 litres (35,000 tons) per day. Or, to put it in more graphic terms, the total amount supplied in the pipelines leading to Reykjavík is roughly equivalent to having two giant lorries deliver water to consumers every other minute of the day and night.

The water used for such consumption has been extensively researched and analysed and is under constant supervision. The supply areas are well guarded and strict security regulations are set up to prevent any degree of pollution. The quality of the water is exceptionally high and the Reykjavík Water Works has collaborated with several companies that specialize in its exportation abroad. The company is also bound by a special analysis system and its own internal inspection regulations. It now complies with ISO9001 standards.

Yet it is one thing to have access to good water and quite another to have a sufficient supply. Research has revealed that the volume of high-quality water in the Reykjavík area is enough to serve up to at least two million consumers. The fresh-water reservoir is, then, a highly valuable asset to the city.

Water for Everyone

Reykjavík is one of the few cities in the industrialised world where it is possible to drink pure, unpolluted water, no matter whether it is taken directly from a household faucet or from the hoses set up for washing cars at Reykjavík's petrol stations.

All the consumers in Reykjavík are well aware of the quality of the water but very few put much time or thought into how to conserve it. Each cubic metre of water, that is to say each ton, that is fed along one of the city's two major pipelines to consumers can be utilised by many people. It has been shown, for example, that each inhabitant uses about

Free and Flying... Each year hundreds of young children attend Reykjavík kindergartens while older children and teenagers flock by the thousands to primary and secondary schools.

124

Vatnsberinn (*"The Water Deliverer" by Ásmundur Sveinsson*) **and the Pearl.** *The people who strove to bring fresh water to old Reykjavík did not even faintly expect that, some day, hot water would be piped directly into homes from tanks like those beneath the Pearl.*

10 litres a day to water the garden and twice that amount for cooking. The large companies, on the other hand, such as those in the fishing industry, the breweries and processors of raw materials can use tens or even hundreds of tons of water a day. Domestic consumers pay for their water in the form of a flat water rate while the companies and institutions basically pay according to volume.

There is only one large fountain in Reykjavík, which spouts attractively from the southern part of Tjörnin. It is supplied by fresh water. There are also a few smaller fountains and various water art works, the best known being *Fyssa* in the botanical gardens at Laugardalur.

An Autumn Evening in Reykjavík. In good weather on a Saturday evening, thousands of people visit the old city centre.

Running Water Changed to Power

Neither the people of Reykjavík nor those in the rest of the country harnessed water as was done elsewhere in Europe before the industrial revolution. For example, the only water mill in Iceland, was built as part of an industrial project in the eighteenth century. There were a few windmills in Reykjavík, but none of them remain today. Iceland had no trains, and steam engines were only found in shipping vessels. There was never any internal waterway system to speak of. Indeed, water was not generally used for driving anything until the advent of hydroelectric power, but as soon as it arrived it was quite clear that it was perfectly suited to Icelandic conditions.

The rivers and streams in the Reykjavík area have mostly disappeared into pipelines and drainage systems. The only large river that remains is the relatively short Elliðaár river with a flow of five tons per second and is a combination of a direct run-off and spring-fed river. It runs from the Elliðaár lake, which itself gathers water from a very large area, including that at Gvendarbrunnar, and runs through a shallow valley down to the sea. A flow of lava covered the area about 5,000 years ago, causing rapids and small waterfalls to form in the river for most of its length. According to the meteorologists, this valley has the best weather in the whole of Reykjavík. The river is also excellent for salmon fishing, a fact first mentioned in documents from the medieval period.

At the end of 1894, initial investigations were made into the prospect of setting up a large water-run electricity plant at the Elliðaár river. The first part of the project was initiated in 1919, but was superseded by a somewhat larger

"From the viewpoint of an architect working in Reykjavík at the turn of a century, I think that there's growth and positive prospects in sight regarding the city's development. In good years, people seize the moment — and the general outlook is one of exciting growth. Fresh views on the future of the city centre and on the planning of the overall Greater Reykjavík area set the pace. This is the time for young and innovative people to act and we should appraise the work of professionals and the municipality, looking towards the future – a new age".

Hlédís Sveinsdóttir, Architect

Water Turned into Light. *More than 70 years ago, the first electric street lights lit up downtown Reykjavík. This is the suburb of Breiðholt today, seen from the town of Kópavogur.*

Reykjavík at Twilight. *The Pearl and Hallgrímskirkja Church rise above the city skyline – but even higher, the mountains of Reykjanesskagi stand like a wall behind the city.*

construction, producing 1 MW, which was put to use in 1921. The plant served about 800 buildings in Reykjavík during its first year. Reykjavík was then lit by electric street lamps and in the eyes of many at the time this was the first sign that it was a real town

The Elliðaár Power Plant was then expanded with more turbines and dynamos to produce a total capacity of 3.16 MW of electricity. A dam had to be erected in the Elliðaár river just opposite the present Árbær district as well as a new control unit at the source of the Elliðaár Lake. A wooden pressure pipeline was then laid from the lower dam to the plant. The Elliðaár Power Plant has been in constant use until recently, but in recent years it has been relieved for a day or two at a time during the winter months. All the original equipment is still there, though various alterations and additions have had to be made to both the dam and the distribution system. As such, this plant is

> *"I do like to reside here in Reykjavík. The city has everything I need, especially a lot of fine book-stores. I am also studying computer science. The weather here is okay – not too hot or cold. Suits people working outdoors in the summer".*
>
> **Arnar Hafsteinsson, Traffic Warden and Student**

Winter Traffic. Icy fog in twilight. When days are only a few hours long, driving conditions can sometimes be tough, bringing traffic to a crawl.

Winter Riding. The Icelandic horse grows long hair in the winter and is not deterred from outdoor activities in the coldest of winters.

one of the oldest hydroelectric stations in Europe, and now incorporates a small museum built to commemorate its own history as well as the history of the age of electricity in Reykjavík. The plant was run from the very beginning by Reykjavík Electricity, which also managed the distribution and sale of all electric power to the whole of the city. The company traditionally produced a good deal of its own power, but now purchases the main part of it from the largest producer of electric power in Iceland, the National Power Company. In 1999, Reykjavík Electricity merged with Reykjavík District Heating to become Reykjavík Energy.

Further Supplies of Electricity

Reykjavík soon required more electricity than the Elliðaár Power Plant could produce. In 1937, a much larger power station was completed at the River Sog which flows out of Lake Þingvallavatn, and in 1948 a reserve power station was built in the Elliðaár Valley, kindled by oil in the event of cold weather spells or other problems. From then until 1964 two other medium size hydroelectric plants were set up at the Sog, boosting the total capacity to 89 MW. Most of this power was used by Reykjavík and the surrounding towns. By this time, the state partly owned the Sog power plants. A joint national and municipal power and distribution company was established in 1965, the above-mentioned National Power Company. This new company immediately began to build further plants, and after the northern town of Akureyri became a shareholder, one power company served the entire country.

The aim of the Reykjavík Electricity Company and the newly formed Reykjavík Power Company is to produce environmentally friendly power as well as to distribute and sell it in the most cost efficient manner. Run at a profit, it serves Reykjavík and all the neighbouring towns with the exception of Hafnarfjörður and Álftanes, or just under 150,000 consumers. In all, the Reykjavík Power Company produces in excess of 700 MW of power if the geothermal energy is included. The total demand for electrical power is about 120 MW and the total amount of energy consumed is almost 700 gigawatt-hours per year. There are about 26,000 domestic cables, almost 30,000 street lamps, 160 km of aerial cables and 500 km of underground mainlines within the city. Each inhabitant uses about 4,800 kilowatt-hours

Fire Eater. There are lots of attractions at the family entertainment park in Laugardalur. A small zoo and exciting performances, for example, draw people to the park on weekends and for special events.

"I'm one of thousands of students who live and study in Reykjavík and I've discovered that everyday life here is exciting. It's a bit special to live in a capital city where you're not lost in a crowd and where you always meet some friend in the street. The city lies close to the ocean and nature. Clean, handsome and peaceful. I like all this very much. Reykjavík is the city of opportunity with its many levels of education and work, and where culture blossoms. I think that Reykjavík is the world's smallest metropolis".

Gunnar Rúnar Gunnarsson, Student

Gott í gogginn ("A Goody in the Beak"). *What a peculiar name for a deli! Reykjavík's restaurant and café scene is highly interesting.*

The View from the Church Tower of Hallgríms-kirkja. *Looking to the north. Most of the houses date from 1890 to 1920.*

a year, a figure that includes private and commercial consumers. Since each kilowatt-hour costs between IKR 6-7, the average family's electric bill is about IKR 2,000-3,000 per month. This is considered relatively inexpensive by foreign standards.

Treasures of Nature

The Elliðaár river became part of Reykjavík in 1906, and with the construction of the small power plant both the valley and the natural environment inevitably underwent considerable change. However, almost immediately, Reykjavík Electricity put into effect plans to preserve the salmon stock in the river and to ensure that the general natural surroundings were as little affected as possible. Salmon fry have been released into the river, and a hatching station has been run there for a long time, either by the town authorities or by the Reykjavík Anglers' Club. The club has sold fishing permits and rights since 1937. The river attracts all kinds of anglers, from the mayor of Reykjavík to the Hollywood star Bing Crosby. Approximately 1,000-2,000 salmon have been caught there each year.

Improvements to the Elliðaár area involve reforestation and the protection of the valley from sewage pollution and over-grazing. From 1951, thousands of trees of varying species have been planted on the flatlands below the dam towards the coastline. The Reykjavík Forestation Association is now in charge of all forestry in that area which now consists of a large blend of trees, bushes and shrubs, interspersed with footpaths and small bridges. Now the entire valley stands as a reminder that town and country need not be separate entities.

Reykjavík and Iceland's lifelines

In a sparsely populated country such as Iceland, internal communications are a key factor and indeed the same may be said of Iceland's communications with the outside world which rendered the country remote for so many centuries. For a very long period, Reykjavík has been the heart of the country's communications.

The first car was imported to Iceland in 1904, but the automobile age did not effectively begin there until nearly two decades later. In 1920, 190 cars were imported and the capital soon became the centre for the rapid development that swept across the industrialised world. The increasing number of cars soon led to radical changes not only in the capital's internal road system but also in its link roads to the rest of the country. In 1935 it took two days to drive to Akureyri in the north of Iceland. Today, the same journey takes five to six hours, and the opening of a 5.7 km tunnel under Hvalfjörður has reduced the journey to the west and north by 50-60 km.

In the inter-war years, Iceland began its first passenger flights, though from 1935 to 1940 this was primarily conducted by small sea-planes flying on a fairly regular basis. The first air stations in Reykjavík were thus effectively harbours rather than airports, situated

The Elliðaár River. *Few (if any) other world capitals can boast of a good salmon river, well within the city limits.*

Reykjavík Airport. The airport was constructed during the Second World War and has served Reykjavík – and Iceland – for decades. Presently, most landings and take-offs fall into domestic commercial traffic and private aviation categories.

at Vatnagarðar and Skerjafjörður. With the construction of the Reykjavík Airport in the Second World War, passenger and freight flights underwent a major change and air travel suddenly became one of the country's main lifelines. The Reykjavík Airport served as the main airfield for over two decades and has always remained the centre for internal flights, now handling between 300,000-400,000 passengers a year as well as a large volume of freight. Moreover, it is conveniently close to the heart of the city. However, for some parties, the location of the airport is a controversial issue, partly for reasons of safety or noise pollution and partly because of the amount of space it takes.

If one looks back over the centuries at the history of Reykjavík and Iceland as a whole, the transport of supplies both around the country and from the outside world by ship has been by far the most important means of communication. In short, the sea has always been the country's major lifeline. However, right through to the end of the medieval period and beyond, the

"I like to live in the Greater Reykjavík area. It's always fun to wake up on a new day. Sometimes I would like to sleep in, though. I want to live only here in the Great Reykjavík area. Regards, Mekkín (the best)".

Ragnheiður Mekkín Ragnarsdóttir, Pupil

Reykjavík harbour was not a major port. But after Germany emerged as the victor over Britain in the battle for Icelandic trade and Iceland's Danish masters later declared a monopoly on the same, Reykjavík gradually became the most important site for the import and export of goods. It was also the main port of call for most visitors to the country. Sailing vessels and then steam ships dropped anchor at the town harbour, and wares and passengers were brought ashore first in row boats and then motor vessels. Stores and warehouses sprung up close to the docks until the first wooden jetties were constructed there at the turn of the nineteenth century. Much of the postal service went to and from Reykjavík by sea.

Improvements and the enlargement of the Reykjavík harbour began just before the First World War, modernising and consolidating the entire area. At that time, a new system of docks and jetties was constructed with a mixture of timber, stone, steel and concrete. When sea traffic increased, the harbour had to be made deeper and a significant amount of land was reclaimed from the sea.

At about the same time, Iceland started its shipping industry and founded its own shipping companies which slowly took over most of the country's operations. The harbour grew busier and busier each year, and from 1920-50 it began to take on the appearance that it has today. It dealt with almost all imports and ran domestic shipping operations to serve the rest of the country. All types of boats and ships, including the then com-

Salted Cod. *Salted Icelandic cod is held in high esteem in the Mediterranean countries where it's called baccalao.*

"The Yellow One". Sustainable fishing is considered the key to Iceland's prosperity. Stocky, mature cod are an important part thereof.

mon but now obsolete side-trawlers unloaded their bountiful catches at the harbour. It was also the centre for commodities which were, to a large extent, brought in by freight ships from harbours all over Iceland. And before air travel took over, the harbour was the most important centre for passenger communications in Iceland.

In the Second World War, the Reykjavík harbour also served a further and rather different role. It became the chief military port for the occupying British forces, who came to Iceland in 1940 to protect the country against a potential German invasion. Co-operation between the occupying forces and the Icelandic government was quick to develop, and to hold when US forces took over from the British in 1941. At this time, not only the harbour but the whole city effectively became a military base.

A new harbour

Seamen's Day. The first Sunday in June each year celebrates the contribution of seamen to the economy and society of Iceland. This hardy gentleman has been decorated for his work.

In 1965, the volume of goods and traffic at the harbour had reached its peak and became too small for all the exported fish products and other goods that were being brought ashore from abroad. Plans were soon put into effect concerning the future of shipping and a large site was chosen further along the coast which came to be known as Sundarhöfn. The said area stretches along the shore from Laugarnes, across Vatnagarðar and as far as the bay at Elliðaár. Hundreds of thousands of tons of freight are landed and loaded at Sundahöfn each year, which also now serves as the main port for the larger cruise ships and other passenger vessels. Close by there is a small marina for leisure boats. Sundarhöfn is still undergoing expansion. A third harbour and adjoining services are likely to be developed in the future at Eiðsvík, between Geldinganes and Gufunes.

The old harbour near the centre of town is still the site of some considerable activity. It is still an important port for both large and small Icelandic and foreign fishing vessels, as well as for tourist trips and cruise ships during the summer months. The large Icelandic trawlers enter the western part of the old harbour to land their catches, as do the one-man vessels. The grey coloured fleet of the Coast Guard and ships belonging to the Marine Research Institute lie close to the harbour entrance. Finally, there are a number of boats that are docked there, such as four disused whaling vessels and a beautiful reconstruction of a Viking long boat, which is used for various occasions. A small shipyard, which only carries out maintenance and painting services is also close to the old harbour as well as a number of companies that deal in goods or services connected with boats and shipping. Nearby Örfirisey, the home of the country's main oil storage tanks is situated, flanked by varying different business and marine services.

As soon as the main weight of imports and exports was moved to Sundahöfn, the old harbour and surrounding area lost some of its importance but very little of its charm. In the nearby streets, not only companies associated with fishing and shipping but various other businesses, services, offices and educational and cultural institutions have appeared, often in the very buildings used for previous harbour activities. The area also has its fair share of restaurants, shops and galleries.

Eimskip. *That is the name of the oldest shipping company in Iceland. Its base is at the new harbour, Sundahöfn. The crane is named Jaki, the nickname of one of Reykjavík's late labour leaders.*

The Eastern Part of Reykjavík. *Miklatún, the public garden at Kjarvalsstaðir (Reykjavík Art Museum) is seen here in the forefront. Mt. Vífilsfell and the Bláfjöll skiing area are seen in the background, some 25 km distant.*

References

Árni Hjartarson. Síðkvarteri jarðlagastaflinn í Reykjavík og nágrenni. Náttúrufræð-ingurinn. Hið íslenska náttúrufræðifélag. Reykjavík 1980.

Eggert Þór Bernharðsson. Saga Reykjavíkur. Borgin 1940-1990. Fyrri og síðari hluti. Iðunn. Reykjavík 1998.

Guðjón Friðriksson. Saga Reykjavíkur. Bærinn vaknar. 1870-1940. Fyrri og síðari hluti. Iðunn. Reykjavík 1991/1994.

Hörður Ágústsson. Íslensk byggingararfleifð I. Ágrip af húsagerðarsögu 1750-1940. Húsafriðunarnefnd ríkisins. Reykjavík 1998.

Ingvar Birgir Friðleifsson. Jarðsaga Esju og nágrennis. Árbók Ferðafélags Íslands. Reykjavík 1985.

Jón Jónsson. Jarðsaga svæðisins milli Selvogsgötu og Þrengsla. Árbók Ferðafélags Íslands. Reykjavík 1985.

Ólafur K. Nielsen (ed.). Tjörnin, saga og lífríki. Reykjavíkurborg. Reykjavík 1992.

Páll Líndal. Reykjavík 200 ára. Hagall. Reykjavík 1986.

Þorleifur Einarsson. Jarðfræði. Mál og menning. Reykjavík 1992.

Ari Trausti Guðmundsson

A free-lance geophysicist and writer, educated in Norway and Iceland. He has been an educator and a writer for more than two decades – the author of numerous books and articles on the subjects of nature, science and research, outdoor activities, environmental issues and mountaineering. Besides having produced and hosted countless radio/television programmes, films and documentaries, Ari Trausti is also one of Iceland's most popular television weathermen. He holds special interest in high mountains, glaciers, volcanism and Arctic/Antarctic exploration and research.

Ragnar Th. Sigurðsson

An independent professional photographer who leads his own company (Arctic Images). Educated in Iceland and Sweden, he has worked as a photographer for over two decades. He specialises in photography for advertising and that of people and nature in Iceland and the Arctic countries. Ragnar has provided a wealth of photographs for books, magazines, annual reports and posters, to mention some examples. He received the Clio Award in 1998 for Poster Pictures. Ragnar is associated with Tony Stone/Getty Images in London. Ari Trausti and Ragnar have together compiled two best-selling books – one about Icelandic glaciers (*Light on Ice*), another about the Vatnajökull eruption in 1996 (*Ice on Fire*).

Contents